...AND WE THOUGHT
THE WAR WAS OVER

David Lee

...and we thought the war was over

DAVID LEE

Illustrated by

RICHARD LEE

Thomas Harmsworth Publishing Company
Stoke Abbott

By the same author:
Never Stop the Engine when it's Hot
(Thomas Harmsworth Publishing, 1983)

Text © 1991 David Lee

Illustrations © 1991 Richard Lee

British Library Cataloguing in Publication Data
Lee, David *1912–*
  – and we thought the war was over.
1. Indonesia. British prisoners of war, history.
Evacuation of British prisoners of war from Indonesia,
history, Great Britain, Royal Air Force. Fighter Command
I. Title
940.54779598

ISBN 0–948807–13–X

Typeset by Fox Design, Surbiton

Printed and bound in Great Britain by
Bookcraft [Bath] Ltd

Author's Note

This is not a history. Although most of the events and incidents did take place in 1945-46, many of the names and certainly the dialogue are fictitious.

The book tells of the experiences and reminiscences of a Group Captain posted to the Far East immediately after VE Day to command a Fighter Wing equipped with the American P 47 Thunderbolt aircraft. My war did not end as was to be expected when Japan capitulated after the delivery of two atomic bombs, but continued for a further year in the East Indies during the work of evacuating thousands of Allied prisoners of war and internees in the face of most intense opposition from Indonesians.

The place names and spelling are those of the period: many have changed since those times, e.g. Batavia is now Djakarta. Readers who had personal knowledge of South East Asia at that time must make allowances when their memory of particular events does not coincide entirely with what I have written.

David Lee

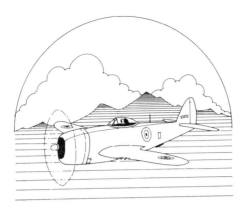

1

Off to the Far East

No work was done that day. The pubs were full to overflowing, Buckingham Palace was besieged by noisy crowds, Downing Street was similarly invested, pretty girls were kissed by total strangers and even taxi drivers gave free rides. For this was 'Victory in Europe' on 8 May, 1945, VE Day. Almost every law in the land must have been broken that day but nobody cared, least of all the police who joined in the celebrations with complete abandon, and history does not record how many policemen's helmets were missing the following day.

No more bombs on London and the provincial cities: no more driving to work over acres of broken glass, with women in their nightclothes wandering aimlessly amid the ruins of their houses. No more packed bodies sleeping on the platforms of underground stations and no more sharing one tin hat with the man from the Prudential with whom I carried out firewatching patrols in Edgware when not on duty in the Air Ministry. We had won, and the boys could all come home and pick up the good jobs which they so richly deserved.

But wait a minute! The Axis Powers may have been defeated but we were still fully engaged in a bitter struggle against the Japanese in South East Asia. The XIVth Army (the forgotten army) had been slogging away in terrible conditions in Burma for years and although the end of that campaign was in sight, the war against Japan was far from over. The British Pacific Fleet was engaged alongside its American colleagues and the RAF was forming a force of Lancaster bombers to go to the Pacific. No, Victory in Europe was one very important step, but it was not the end of the war by any means. The boys could not all come home and, furthermore, thousands of additional soldiers, sailors and airmen had to go out to join them in the Far East.

It turned out that I was to be one of those thousands, and to some extent it was my own fault – if fault it can be called. As a young Group Captain I had, for the past two years or so, been 'polishing a mahogany bomber' as Deputy Director of Plans in the Air Ministry and the Cabinet Offices. Throughout the planning and execution of the operation to invade Europe, there had been no respite for the planners and so, on returning from the Quebec and Yalta Conferences early in 1945, I approached my Director of Plans.

'I wonder, sir, if you would consider recommending me for a job in the fresh air, possibly in command of a unit involving some flying. I am beginning to feel a bit jaded and am certainly out of flying practice.'

Air Commodore 'Tubby' Dawson thought for a few moments and then said, 'Yes, David, I think you have deserved a break. Victory seems to be in sight and you need some command experience to balance up all the staff work you've done lately. But,' he added 'it may mean going to the Far East, which is the only theatre where the action is likely to continue.' 'Well,' I said, 'I have had one full tour in India already, and have some

2

experience of South East Asia so that a posting there wouldn't seem inappropriate.'

Tubby was as good as his word and a few weeks later he told me he had been able to arrange a posting to the Far East and, he said, 'I believe you will get an appointment in command, but of what or where I cannot even guess: that will be a matter for the Commander-in-Chief out there. However, you will go with a strong recommendation from here, and I hope they will give you something worthwhile.'

Sentence had been passed. Doubts immediately began to assail me. Had I been right to initiate this step, knowing full well that it would mean leaving Denise and our two small children behind as all postings overseas were, of course, unaccompanied while the war continued? From a career point of view – and I was a regular officer with a permanent commission – it made sense, but the severance of family ties for several years would be traumatic. However, the die had been cast, and the family accepted it with understanding.

VE day came as I was making my final preparation to fly out, the 18th of May being the date of departure. Although going into the tropics at the beginning of the hot weather, there was not much kitting-out that I could do, the baggage allowance being a miserly 44lbs, very different to the cabin trunks I had taken to India in 1933. 'Don't worry,' I was told, 'you can easily get all you want out there.' Basically this turned out to be right except for some important items such as a Group Captain's gold braided hat.

The days rushed past amid a good deal of family unhappiness while everybody around us was wildly celebrating the great victory. Denise and I decided to have a farewell lunch at the Café Royal before she was to see me off to Lyneham by train to catch my aircraft. It was a disaster. While eating our lunch Denise had placed her fur stole on the back of her chair. When we rose to go it had disappeared. The Café Royal was turned upside down, waiters were questioned and the manager called, but all to no avail. No sign of it could be found and time to catch

3

my train at Paddington was getting short. 'We must report it to the police,' I said to the manager and, of course, he agreed.

We walked disconsolately up Regent Street into Vine Street police station. The police were sympathetic and helpful, promising to investigate at the Café Royal, but clearly did not hold out much hope of finding it or the culprit. I had to go, as my train left Paddington at 4 o'clock in order to book in at Lyneham that evening. I left Denise sitting there miserably and that was the last we were to see of each other for more than eighteen months.

After a sleepless night during which I rang home to find, as I expected, that there were no developments about the fur stole, the Avro York rumbled down the Lyneham runway at 5.30 am with some forty RAF passengers, none of whom seemed happy either to be returning to continue an overseas tour or, like myself, starting one. There was, however, one congenial soul, Group Captain Max Perkins, an Engineer officer on his way to Singapore. Throughout the four long, vibrating days of the flight to Colombo, we consoled each other suitably at each night stop. The York was a masterpiece of compromise – the wings and engines of the Lancaster bomber attached to a large square box for the passengers. Sturdy and reliable it may have been, but nobody could call it comfortable for four or five days on end, and that was the time it took to fly from England to Singapore. On the fourth evening, after a flight lasting 29 hours, I disembarked at Colombo and was put up at the Galleface Hotel which had virtually become a transit camp.

To my great surprise I found that I was expected and the next day was despatched up to Kandy where the Supreme Allied Commander, Lord Mountbatten and Air Chief Marshal Sir Keith Park had their headquarters. The trip by road through Ceylon with its plantations and luxuriant vegetation, climbing eventually into the cooler air of Kandy, was a great pleasure after the discomforts of the long flight from home.

Amid the temples and pagodas which symbolize Kandy, a terrible shambles of huts and odd buildings made up the South

East Asia Command headquarters. All was bustle and activity: Rangoon had been captured on 3rd May and it was hoped that the Burma campaign was virtually over. Even so, Sir Keith had time for a few words with me. A very tall, austere man who had had a great reputation during the Battle of Britain, he welcomed me to his office. 'I know what you have been doing for the past few years,' he said, 'and I have been asked to give you a good command if possible: well, I think it will be possible, and we have in mind for you one of the tactical Wings in Paddy Bandon's 224 Group which is just withdrawing from Burma and setting up shop at Bangalore.'

This was excellent news, and I thanked him warmly. 'Before reporting to Bandon you must go up to Delhi and complete the necessary administrative details. You will be going to a very fine Group which has fought with great distinction in Burma, and I wish you every success.'

I returned in high spirits to Colombo and was lucky enough to get a seat in a Liberator bound for Delhi the next day with just enough time to get my meagre stock of tropical uniform washed. I could already see that keeping a clean and neat uniform for all the reporting to senior officers was going to be a problem, but so far so good.

It was a long flog of eight hours, incarcerated in the belly of the Liberator – a standard bomber with few concessions to passengers. At Delhi the heat hit me like the blast from a furnace when the doors were opened. The small hotel was comfortable enough and, after a cold shower, I wandered into the garden where a slightly cooler evening breeze was moving the palm leaves. In the middle of the lawn was a deck chair with its back to me and, as I strolled towards it, a pungent cloud of tobacco smoke drifted up from it. That sight and that smell told me exactly who the occupant was. I crept up and said, 'Uncle, what are you doing here?'

The occupant choked on his pipe and burst into a paroxysm of coughing. It was 'Uncle' Ray who had been my Army colleague in the Cabinet Office. When he recovered, it turned out that he had been posted to an appointment in India and was waiting to be on his way. He was a good deal older that I was and had a slow and deliberate manner. Never will I forget an occasion when our Naval planning colleague made some far fetched suggestion about the use of the British fleet in the Pacific. Uncle had paused, taken his pipe slowly out of his mouth and said, 'Tony, I don't agree with you, I can't agree with you and whatever you say, I won't agree with you.' This brought that particular discussion to an end! Meeting 'Uncle' Ray ensured a pleasant and nostalgic evening when I was beginning to feel decidedly lost in the vast administrative complex which Delhi had become.

On the following morning I reported to Base Air Forces South East Asia, the somewhat grandiose name by which the huge headquarters which administered all the RAF in Sir Keith Park's command went under. As I expected, nobody had heard of me, but when I mentioned my interview with Sir Keith, much searching of files and telegrams eventually brought my name to light. 'I am sure you will understand,' I was told, 'Rangoon has just fallen and we have a highly complicated withdrawal from Burma to organize.' I did understand and sympathised with the problems ahead of BAFSEA, particularly in that heat which is quite unrelenting in Delhi at the end of May.

As I was apparently destined for an operational Wing, I needed to be kitted-out with 'Jungle Green'. Jungle Green uniform was in use throughout the operational areas of Burma for obvious reasons of camouflage. It was tough, serviceable and, most important, did not show the dirt like khaki drill. Furthermore, a well cut bush jacket could look very smart. The problem of a Group captain's gold braided hat then arose. I felt that I must have a spare one but none was available in the clothing stores. 'However,' they said, 'go into the bazaar to Ghulam Mahomed; he makes Service caps and should be able to fix you up.'

I found a tonga – a two wheeled horse and trap – and, with much ringing of bells and cursing of pedestrians by the driver, I was eventually delivered to a seedy shop in the middle of the bazaar. 'Yes, of course,' said Mr Ghulam Mahomed, 'make many good hats for Group Captain sahibs.' There were no examples for me to inspect and I had no option but to order one, for which I was duly measured. Then arose the difficulty of where to send it, having no idea as yet where I would finish this trek around the sub-continent. The answer seemed to be to send it 'care of 224 Group' at Bangalore, and this was agreed after the exchange of 200 Rupees – a good deal less than Gieves would have charged. But I had fairly serious doubts about this hat as the tonga wallah thrashed his wretched horse back to my hotel.

That evening in the Mess I met Group Captain Denis David of the 224 Group operations staff and related the story of my hat. He roared with laughter, saying, 'Well, you'll certainly get a Group Captain's hat but I doubt whether it would be acceptable on parade at Uxbridge. Many of us have Ghulam Mahomed's caps and a very peculiar collection they are. Not to worry, we are not very dress conscious in the Group and they give the troops a good laugh. Unfortunately we don't wear bush hats any longer outside Burma. Incidentally,' he continued, 'I think you are going to get 904 Wing, lucky so and so. It's a Thunderbolt Wing of four squadrons and is just withdrawing from the Arakan (Burma) where it has performed extremely well for a long time. Maybe I shouldn't have told you this but I'm pretty sure you'll hear it from the AOC in the next few days.'

This was the first definite indication of my fate and it rocked me back on my heels for a moment. Command of a fighter Wing of four squadrons – eighty aircraft, no less. Having been brought up as a bomber pilot my only experience of fighters had been two short trips in a Spitfire. However, this was no time to show any surprise and certainly no doubts to Denis, who was a well known Battle of Britain veteran. Pressing another Muree beer into my hand, he went on, 'I'm flying back to Bangalore tomorrow; come with me and enjoy the luxury of a Beechcraft.' I gratefully accepted this invitation as no arrangements had so far been made for me to get back to 224 Group.

7

Seven o'clock the next morning saw us taxi-ing out in the Beech, a twin engined American aircraft seating about eight passengers. We were alone in it and Denis generously invited me to fly it. 'You probably need the practice and I get almost too much,' he said. It was a pleasant aircraft to fly; the weather was perfect giving the prospect of another sweltering day over central India and we made good time to Nagpur where we landed to refuel and have a late breakfast after three hours. The second half of the flight was equally uneventful and I touched down at Bangalore after a further three hours. After the parched look of most of central India the city looked most attractive, quite green and well tree'd with large numbers of brilliant flame trees dotted about. As we circled Denis pointed out the tented headquarters of 224 Group on a barren patch just outside. 'You will have to stay in a hotel,' he shouted, 'we have no spare accommodation for visitors, but you'll be more comfortable than in a tent.'

Bangalore was much cooler than Delhi for which I was grateful. After travelling almost the length of India three times in the last week and then getting six hours unaccustomed flying practice, I was weary. The hotel had mosquito nets and no need for fans. A rudimentary knowledge of Urdu, learned on the North West Frontier almost ten years earlier was coming in very handy during these travels.

On Denis's advice I dressed the following morning in my new jungle green bush jacket and slacks and was picked up by car to be taken out to the headquarters. 224 Group had only been out of Burma for a few weeks but the layout of the tents was quite smart, revealing years of experience of setting up camp in far less salubrious surroundings than Bangalore. I was directed along to the tent of the Air Officer i/c Administration (AOA) and come face to face with Bernard Chacksfield. 'Good God, Chacks, how did you manage to become an Air Commodore?' He had been in my junior term as a cadet. 'It won't last,' he replied, 'everything is a bit odd out here, and when this lot is over I shall doubtless come down with a bump.' How right he was: sometime later he dropped two ranks when I dropped one and we both finished up as Wing Commanders. 'Come along and meet Paddy Bandon.'

Air Vice-Marshal the Earl of Bandon commanded 224 Group and had done so for some time. He was an Irish peer and variously known as 'Paddy' to his friends and 'the abandoned earl' to others. He was one of the great characters of the Royal Air Force; an extrovert and a fine leader who was immensely respected by all who served under him. Like many great leaders he needed a thoroughly efficient staff to handle the administrative and technical details of his command. He made me very welcome.

'Come to get your knees brown and sand in your crutch, have you?' he asked, smoking a cigarette with strange little puffs which I soon found to be a well known habit. In fact all his movements and his frequent loud laugh were both spasmodic and quick. 'Well,' he continued, 'I've decided to give you command of 904 Wing which is on its way out of Burma, equipped with Mosquitos.' 'Excuse me, sir,' I said, interrupting him, 'but I thought 904 Wing had Thunderbolts.' 'Oh,' he said and paused for some time, looking up at a large chart on an easel in front of his desk. Then he laughed loudly. 'Of course it is – Thunderbolts. Anyway, it's a fine Wing which has done wonderful work in the Arakan – four squadrons altogether, so you'll have eighty aircraft to cope with. 224 Group has taken over a string of airfields down the east coast, from south of Calcutta almost to Ceylon and I have allocated the two southern ones to 904 Wing, Ulunderpet and Tanjore. These airfields, which are all unoccupied, were built several years ago against the possibility of the Japanese invading India. As we have now recaptured Burma that threat has disappeared. We have to use them to prepare ourselves to assault Malaya and retake Singapore. As you were a planner, you are probably aware of this.' 'Yes I am , sir, – Operation Zipper.' 'Fine,' he said, 'you probably know more about the plan than I do, which could be useful. At the moment we hope to mount Zipper in September but it will mean a great deal of hard work to re-equip the force after the mauling it's had in the jungle. Well, that's your job and I'm sure you will find it quite a challenge. Just one thing before you tackle it . . . ' He paused and looked searchingly at me in my smart new uniform. 'Your men have had a hard and uncomfortable time during the last year or two. Don't be too hard on them and give them as much freedom as you can. Re-equip them and clean them up but don't introduce too much 'bull'. They are nearly all wartime airmen – civilians in uniform – and you will find very few regulars among them. They all want to go home, but the war isn't over yet and they'll need a firm hand with a gentle touch. Come up here whenever you want help or advice and I shall drop in to see you quite informally from time to time. Any Questions?'

I was rather bemused by this quick fire briefing and began to understand the personality of my new AOC. The latest story I had heard about him was that he had quite recently walked down Piccadilly and into the RAF Club dressed in bush jacket, shorts and a bush hat, to the astonishment of the club members. Some years later, when he was a senior NATO commander at Fontainebleau he sat in a huge, bare office with only two small framed pictures on the walls. Behind him was a document containing the official displeasure of the Air Council for sending an RAF Regiment Squadron to quell a riot on Gan island in the Indian Ocean contrary to instructions. Facing him in this large office was a framed motto, 'I love my work; I can sit and look at it for hours on end.' These anecdotes seemed to me to sum up Paddy Bandon's personality.

He invited me to the tented Mess that evening after taking me round the various office tents to meet the members of his staff, on whom I could already see I was going to rely heavily in the coming months if the disquieting stories about the withdrawal from Burma were true. I sensed a slight feeling of jealousy that a young Group Captain, fresh from home, should be taking over one of the tactical Wings for the forthcoming push towards Singapore, but everybody was most friendly and it was probably my imagination. Anyway, I was offered a small Fairchild Argus to fly myself to Ulunderpet the following day with a Sergeant Pilot to bring the aircraft back. With much to think about and full of good cheer, I retired to my hotel, looking forward to an early start to my new command. Little did I know that it would be the last comfortable night I would spend for a long time.

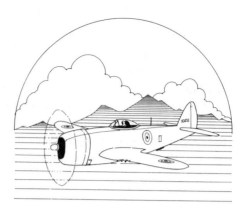

2

Ulunderpet

On 8th June, only two weeks after leaving home (although it seemed much longer) I was on my way to Ulunderpet: a strange un-Indian sounding name, the origin or meaning of which I never discovered (although I formed an opinion after a while there that in any language it meant 'God, what an awful place!')

A Sergeant Pilot named Williams was to accompany me in the Argus, for which I was grateful as he was an experienced Argus Pilot and I was, after all, very much out of practice. The Argus was a trim little high wing monoplane, many of which were in use by the RAF for short range communications throughout South East Asia. It seated four people in two pairs and boasted a modest cruising speed of 110 mph.

Williams explained the essentials to me and we set off at 7 o'clock on a fine, bright morning which was obviously going to turn into a 'scorcher'. 'I should go up to about 5000 feet if I were you, sir,' said Williams, 'there is virtually no wind, and you'll get a good view of the countryside – for what it's worth,' he added. I soon saw what he meant as we left the green oasis of Bangalore behind and flew to the east.

As the little aeroplane hummed quietly along Williams kept up an interesting description of the various landmarks, such as the Hindustan aircraft factory which was one of India's fairly recent technical successes. The countryside became more and more flat and uninteresting, clearly lacking in water and beginning to suffer from the parching effects of the hot weather. Ulunderpet lay about 150 miles south east of Bangalore, not all that far from the old French colonial settlement of Pondicherry and the east coast.

We ploughed on for about an hour and a half when Williams said, 'You'll soon see the runway which is about eight miles ahead.' I began a gentle descent and, within minutes, a long concrete runway began to take shape. As we approached, it appeared to be totally isolated in a vast patch of scrubland. At about 1000 feet I levelled out and looked around. 'There seems to be a village of sorts over there,' I said, pointing to the left. 'No, that is your domestic site, messes, living quarters, etc.' I looked to the right and there was another untidy collection of thatched huts which Williams told me was the technical site. I couldn't believe it; the place seemed to cover about 20 miles. Circling slowly round, I then saw that there were quite a lot of concrete hard standings close to the runway and about half a dozen Thunderbolts parked on them with various thatched buildings near the western end of the runway. 'Those are the flying wing and squadron headquarters,' I was told. 'No wonder Paddy Bandon had not been more specific about what I would find. I turned to Williams. 'Before we land I would like to have a look at Tanjore, my second airfield. How far is it?' Williams studied his map. 'About fifty or sixty miles due south,' he finally said, and I turned off to the right, starting to climb back to 5000 feet, more to avoid the increasing heat than anything else.

Tanjore turned out to be much like Ulunderpet, one long concrete runway of about 2000 yards with similar dispersal sites, although in this case they were not quite so widely separated and there was a sizeable village nearby. Tanjore was completely deserted as we slowly circled round – no Thunderbolts and, as far as I could see, no sign of life.

As we flew north again I said, 'Well Sergeant Williams, it looks as though I have a job of work on my hands!' Too true, sir,' he replied, 'but better than Burma, and you have to remember that all these airfields were built several years ago and the dispersal was designed at that time to limit damage from Japanese attacks.' We had dispersed at home, notably in the early days of the war, but nothing on the scale of what I had seen in the last hour or so. Pictures of airmen having to walk three miles to work in the heat of an Indian summer came to my mind. I felt pretty depressed as I flew round Ulunderpet and, to my surprise received a green Aldis lamp signal from the end of the runway before landing. The runway was concrete, reasonably smooth and undamaged in spite of its lack of use for some years. But I did notice that it was unfenced and several herds of goats and 'shoats' (a cross between a sheep and a goat) were wandering about in the scrub close to the runway, tended by young children or very old men.

As I stepped out of the Argus, I was met with a smart salute from a young Squadron Leader. He introduced himself. 'George Rumsey, sir. I am your SAdO (Senior Administrative Officer) and very glad to see you. Welcome to 904 Wing.' I took to George at once and although I wasn't to know it at the time, he became one of my mainstays for the next eighteen months. He had arrived in a battered looking Ford V8 saloon, roughly camouflaged with black and green paint. 'I'm afraid this is your car,' he said apologetically. 'It's had a very hard life in Burma and you'll probably find a jeep more reliable and even more comfortable as I think the springs have gone on this thing.'

After a couple of airmen, burned black by the sun and stripped to the waist, had dumped my luggage in the Ford we set off for the domestic site and the mess. We jolted our way over two miles of unmade road to the living quarters and George briefly explained the situation. 'Most of the Wing staff have arrived and the aircraft you saw are the first half of 258 Squadron. The second half, with Neil Cameron the CO, should arrive tomorrow but don't count on it; the withdrawal from Burma is quite chaotic. Everything has to come out through Calcutta and there is an appalling shambles in the docks there. 131 Squadron under Squadron Leader Ford should follow 258, and then 60 and 261 Squadrons will go direct to Tanjore. We do have water, power and some telephones. It's all very primitive but much better than Burma' – (a remark I was beginning to get used to) – 'and I think we can make ourselves reasonably comfortable.'

By this time we were driving slowly through the domestic area which was entirely of basha construction. Bashas of various sizes were built of bamboo poles covered with palm leaves laced onto the bamboo. There was one problem with those huts, which had not been used for two years, and then for only a short period: the thatch had become infested with every imaginable sort of insect – scorpions, tree rats, beetles, mosquitos and even snakes and the roofs became alive at night, which was most disconcerting, I was told. However, our medical officer had already instituted a vigorous programme of DDT spraying and we had apparently been promised by Delhi a Dakota to spray the whole of Ulunderpet and Tanjore from the air.

The Officer's mess was a fairly large basha with a verandah running round it supported by wooden pillars. I was surprised on entering it to see how comfortable it was. Rush matting covered the floor and the usual issue bamboo furniture seemed to have reached Ulunderpet somehow. The Wing headquarters staff had done wonders in the brief time since they arrived and their own comment was that, with all its drawbacks, the station was much better than anything they had lived in for the past year.

As we lunched on the inevitable tough chicken curry, which immediately took me back to my first tour in India ten years before, I said, 'You all realise, of course, that I have not yet taken the Wing over. Where is the CO incidentally?' There was a short silence broken by Lawrence, the Adjutant. 'I have a telegram for you from him, sir,' handing me the piece of paper. It was from Calcutta and suggested that I should go up there and take the Wing over officially from my predecessor in the Grand Hotel. I couldn't believe my eyes, and read the telegram again amid an awkward silence. 'What is the CO doing in the Grand Hotel?' I asked. Another pause and somebody said that they thought he was on leave. I opened my mouth to make some comment but shut it again quickly. I was beginning to see what lay behind some of the remarks made by Paddy Bandon during my interview with him. 'Right,' I said, 'I'll reply to it when I've had a look round. I must say that you seem to have done extremely well in setting up the station for the squadrons to come in. Incidentally, where is the Wing Commander?' I knew that Wing Commander Whitehead was the Wing Commander Flying but I had never met him. George Rumsey answered. 'He is still in the Arakan arranging the packing up and departure of the squadrons. He should be here in a few days.'

I spent the rest of the day bouncing round the station in a jeep, inspecting all the sections and chatting to the troops who, despite the rough and ready conditions, were very cheerful and mightily relieved to be out of the jungle. They were full of questions about the future and the chances of getting home, none of which I could answer other than to say that Japan was not defeated, but I hoped there would be a few months of rest for them before the next slice of action. Almost without exception the airmen looked weary – even exhausted – in spite of their deep tan, and it was clear that I must give the highest priority to arranging all the recreation, rest and entertainment possible. Fortunately 904 was a 'mobile' Wing, which meant that it was entirely self contained with transport, tentage, communications equipment, a field hospital and everything needed for it to move anywhere without outside help. That was the theory but, as I was soon to discover, Burma had taken a heavy toll of its mobility, and it was nowhere near as self-supporting as its name implied. Nevertheless by the end of this first trip round, George and I reckoned that Ulunderpet and Tanjore could be made quite comfortable if we could obtain the facilities we needed.

'Time, I think George, to reply to that telegram from Calcutta,' I said as I sat for the first time in my palm leaf and bamboo office with an assortment of small animals scampering through the roof. When written, the telegram stated that I had no intention of taking over the Wing in Calcutta, but I would prepare the necessary documents and await the CO's arrival at Ulunderpet. It was already quite clear to me that, with the piecemeal evacuation from Burma in progress, it was going to be impossible to do a thorough check of the accounts and inventories which was the normal procedure. I need not have worried. Paddy Bandon was a most understanding commander and appreciated that normal peacetime procedures could not possibly apply during the transfer of his units from the mêlée of Burma to the comparative calm of India. To cut a long story short, a somewhat disgruntled Group Captain flew in a few days later: I had the necessary handover documents ready and we signed and he departed back to Calcutta the same day.

I was now the official CO of 904 Wing, and it was time to take stock of our situation and try to get the squadrons fully operational in the next three months, ready for the expected assault on Malaya in September. The remainder of 258 Squadron had arrived under their CO, Squadron Leader Neil Cameron. Little did I know when I met this ebullient officer that he was destined to reach the highest appointment in all three Services – Chief of the Defence Staff – and be elevated to the Peerage. 131 Squadron flew in from Calcutta, more or less in one piece, a few days later, and Ulunderpet was quite a sight with forty Thunderbolts and a couple of Harvards packed on the dispersal standings. 60 and 261 Squadrons had not yet reached Tanjore but were due at any moment.

With the influx of all these aircraft and airmen an ugly rumour was beginning to reach me, namely, that all the airmen's tool kits and much technical equipment had either been stolen or sunk in Calcutta harbour. The rumour turned into fact when I called my heads of sections together with the squadron commanders and my Wing Commander Flying, who had flown our Wing Thunderbolt in with the last arrivals. By some quirk of the Customs Authorities airmen were not permitted to bring their personal tool kits through Calcutta themselves. Much had been stolen or lost in a freighter which had sunk in the Bay of Bengal. Bill Brown, the Engineering Officer, said, 'We have virtually no Thunderbolt tools in any of the squadrons, and most of the aircraft are now unserviceable. A few items may eventually turn up but, having seen the shambles in Calcutta docks with everybody fighting their way out of Burma, I wouldn't bet on it.'

I was appalled. The Thunderbolt was an American aircraft obtained under Lend/Lease conditions and specialist tools would be extremely hard to find in India, as many of them had no commonality with British equipment. But worse was to come.

My senior Equipment Officer, Flight Lieutenant Nichols, then spoke up: 'I'm afraid the same applies to a whole range of equipment. For example, we are desperately short of long range fuel tanks for the aircraft, and they will certainly be needed for any future operations.' A long silence ensued. 'Well,' I said at last, 'we have the inside of three months to get eighty Thunderbolts fully ready for whatever is in store, and I can't possibly tell 224 Group that it's impossible, so what do we do?'

'A suggestion, sir,' said Bill Brown somewhat hesitantly. 'There are very large railway workshops at Trichinopoly and I believe I could persuade them to make at least some basic tools for us, spanners, etc. If you will provide me with a pilot to fly down in one of the Harvards, I will see what can be done.'

Nichols then joined in. 'Similarly, I would like to be flown round the various Maintenance Units in India and liberate,

18

borrow or even steal whatever I can lay my hands on.' I didn't know it at the time but this was the beginning of a most remarkable re-equipment programme which, in more peaceful circumstances, would undoubtedly have resulted in several courts martial – including my own.

'Now, what about transport; will it all be in the same state as my Ford?' I was told that, as a mobile Wing, we had a lot of vehicles of all kinds, from jeeps to fire tenders, and three tonners to cranes, but the condition in which they would arrive was anybody's guess as they had all taken a tremendous beating in the Arakan. 'However,' said my transport officer cheerfully, 'India is stuffed full of vehicles and I don't think it should be too difficult to make good our losses and replace the more clapped out transport. Most of our vehicles are now on their way from Calcutta by road, apart from a few which are being shipped across to Madras, probably from Chittagong. They will all be loaded with our stuff, so there's no danger of losing that in Calcutta docks.'

I had reports from every specialist in turn and the stories were much the same but it was already obvious that the Wing staff was keen and energetic, anxious to get the squadrons fully equipped once more. The only somewhat despondent officer was the accountant. He was dealing in at least half a dozen different currencies and confessed that any sort of audit would probably spell the end of his career. 'I must go up to Delhi fairly soon and sort things out. However the troops are being paid and that is the most important thing.' I told him how understanding 224 Group was and that I would certainly support him in any difficulties. 'I haven't been able to check anything in taking over the Wing,' I said, 'so we are both in the same boat.'

We all repaired to the mess for a few rounds of John Collins and the future began to look much more encouraging than it had a couple of hours earlier. We even had local fish from Pondicherry for dinner that evening instead of the usual curry. I walked to my hut swinging my hurricane lamp that night in a much more cheerful frame of mind.

My hut was a large basha with one room and a tin bath at one end of it, situated about two hundred yards from the mess and out in front of the camp – a very isolated position. I began to hate the eerie walk each night to my lonely bedroom, alive with every kind of living creature. Indeed, one night, as I put my head down, the pillow moved and I ejected from the bed in a flash. Looking cautiously with my torch, I found a snake between the pillow and the case. What kind of snake it was I don't know, but I hurled the lot through the door onto the verandah.

Some nights later I was awakened by the sound of water slopping about outside. I got out of bed and slowly lifted the bamboo and palm leaf flap which served as a window and peered out. It was bright moonlight and there, drinking out of my red fire bucket, was a tiger. Fascinated, I watched it for several minutes until it raised its head, looked around and ambled off across the scrub. Making sure that my revolver was beside me and loaded, I returned to bed, but not to sleep. I'm not a particularly nervous person but I learned to loathe that basha with its nightly visitors.

By the time everybody was working on building up the squadrons again it was 24th June and the hottest time of the year, with the midday temperature climbing beyond the 100° mark and virtually no rain. We worked the old Indian routine of 6 am to 1 pm, with the exception that our limited transport made it impossible to take all the airmen back to the domestic site for breakfast at, say, 8 o'clock. They had to breakfast before starting work which made for a long morning but with a good break in the middle when the ubiquitous 'char wallah' would go round with tea, cakes and cool drinks.

It was high time I got to know the Thunderbolt and I asked Neil Cameron to give me the necessary instruction in its mysteries. I had already taken one of the Harvards up two or three times, a type with which I was reasonably familiar.

The 26th June was a bright clear morning as we walked out to a 258 Squadron T-bolt (to give it its usual name).'Once you get it off the ground, you'll love it,' said Neil. 'It's very easy to fly but is heavy and lands quite fast: bring it in at 110 and put it firmly on the deck and it won't bounce.'

We went over the controls in the cockpit which had two features strange to me. There were two throttles, one normal one for the engine and one for an exhaust driven supercharger located in the tail. 'Before taking off,' said Neil, 'you lock these two throttles together and use them as one until back on the ground again. Secondly, there is water/methanol injection which gives a big boost at take off. You put it in,' pointing to a switch, 'about half way down the runway and away she goes. Both these things are essential with a full load. You'll be very lightly loaded but it is important to make this an automatic drill at all times.' Neil kept his instructions to the minimum for this, my first solo in a Thunderbolt, and I settled down in the roomy cockpit and started up the 2000 horsepower Wright Cyclone engine, closing the bubble canopy.

At the end of the runway, I received permission to take off from our air traffic control which was now in full working order. The punch from the powerful engine was very satisfying as we gathered speed but she seemed reluctant to develop any lift. I pressed the water injection switch as instructed and there was certainly a surge of power but no tendency to lift off. At an indicated 110, I pulled the stick back quite firmly and we staggered into the air. The wheels came up quickly and I started to climb, but she still felt sluggish. At 1000 feet I looked around the cockpit and there was my trouble: I had forgotten to connect the two throttles. Moving the supercharger lever up and locking it to the main throttle transformed the T-bolt and we climbed away and were at 5000 feet within a couple of minutes. I had learned a lesson which I was never to forget.

The P47 Thunderbolt was designed as a high altitude fighter with an official top speed of 440mph at 29,000 feet. The RAF, however, had to use it in South East Asia as a very powerful ground attack aircraft, using its eight 0.5″ guns, bombs and rockets. With long range tanks it was capable of flying at least

1000 miles and delivering a formidable load of weapons. Consequently it was not quite as misused as it may sound and experience in Burma had demonstrated what a punch it could pack.

For half an hour I flew quietly around getting to know the aeroplane and its various controls, going as far as Pondicherry where the old French colonial style buildings stood out in the sunshine. The sea was clear and blue, inviting a visit there as soon as I could find the time.

Now for the first landing, always an interesting moment. One thing disturbed me as I descended towards the airfield: a quiet grumbling, muttering sound kept coming from the rear behind my head, as if an airman was trapped in the tail and talking to himself. Everything seemed to be in order as far as I could tell and so I obtained permission to land. The aircraft was beautifully steady and stable during the approach at 120 and I eased back to 110 as instructed when crossing the threshold. Closing both throttles this time, I put it firmly onto its wheels and, as Neil had said, there was no tendency to bounce – a fast, but very pleasant and easy aircraft to land. 'Now,' I thought to myself, 'I had better do it again with both throttles this time.' The difference was quite marked and, with water injection switched in, we sailed off the runway for a second satisfactory circuit.

'Well done, sir. Did you enjoy it?' said the Corporal who helped me climb rather clumsily down from the cockpit. 'Yes, very much,' I replied, 'but tell me, what is the grumbling noise in the tail at intervals?' He laughed. 'That's the supercharger talking to itself when you aren't using it and it's idling. Open the throttle and it stops as it gets on with its job.' That explained that small mystery. As I dumped parachute and kit in the squadron office Neil Cameron said, 'The first take off was a bit sluggish but both landings were fine.' I had to admit that I had forgotten to link up the throttles but had learned the lesson.

'We've probably all done it at some time, but not with a full load or on a short runway; the same applies to the water injection. If it fails to work, you've got about two seconds in which to decide to jam on the brakes and hope to stop – that's to say with a good load on.'

I returned to my office, feeling that another hurdle had been surmounted, but one thing worried me – the danger of animals on the unfenced runway. I had noticed them within a hundred yards when coming in to land. Wing Commander Whitehead and I discussed it and he made the good suggestion that we build a small pound in the scrubland and drive wayward animals into it, padlock it, and make the herdsmen report to the control tower to get their animals released. We wouldn't fine the villagers: they were too poor anyway, but hope to deter them and keep at least two hundred yards away from the runaway. This we did a few days later and put up a notice in Ulunderpet village. We continued to have some trouble, but after a few goats had been impounded, the herdsmen gave the runway a wide berth and we had few further problems. Nevertheless it remained a worry for the controllers until we left.

The village consisted of little more than a collection of hovels strung out along a very rough road. The villagers were very poor and scratched a living from their herds augmented with a few sparse crops from the poor soil. Our occupation of the airfield was popular as we managed to employ a certain amount of local labour. It was unskilled but honest, which was exactly what we needed. We paid them slightly more than the customary low wages, helped to repair their broken machinery, transported them backwards and forwards as well as making the odd small gift to their community.

June drew to a close – an excessively hot one – and the results of the forays by Nichols, Brown and others began to be seen. A useful load of rough but very acceptable tools came up from the railway workshops which, together with those which began to arrive in our own vehicles from Burma, enabled about half of the Thunderbolts to be flown. With a little more than two months to go to the expected operation, things were looking up and I, for one, began to feel much happier about our chances of getting the Wing back to full operational status.

23

3

Operational Once More

We were now in the middle of India's hot weather, in one of the driest regions of the country. Day after day the sun blazed down from a cloudless sky and the temperature soared to and beyond the 100° mark. It was too hot even for flies and mosquitoes until night fell, when the temperature dropped to a reasonable 80° or so and the mosquitoes came out with the myriads of insects and small animals. Fortunately it was a very dry heat and provided that plenty of salt tablets, which were placed on every mess table, were taken with anti-malarial Mepacrine pills, the conditions were tolerable. The health of the airmen remained remarkably good, which was probably due to the acclimatisation most of them had received in Burma where conditions had been infinitely worse. Bush hats, dirty shorts and chaplis (sandals) were the sole working garments of the airmen with NCOs often painting their stripes on their bare arms in order to maintain some degree of respect. I shudder to think what would have happened had I called for a Wing parade under these circumstances, I even found the Station Warrant Officer, who was of course responsible for discipline, flat on his back one day helping to change a Thunderbolt engine. By way of apology he said, 'I used to work in a car factory, sir, and the boys were having a bit of difficulty with this engine.' He was, however, still wearing his badge of rank strapped round his wrist, covered in oil. 'Well done, Mr James, don't try and salute in that position, you might do yourself an injury.'

July was a month of intense activity in spite of the heat and discomfort. Stores and equipment, not to mention vehicles, began to flow in from all over India, thanks mainly to the extraordinary efforts of Flight Lieutenant Nichols, who by this time, had called upon most of the Maintenance Units in India, leaving them wondering where much of their equipment had gone. The climax of his efforts came when a signal reached me from him saying 'Send six three tonners to Madras on 12 July to meet goods train carrying 100 long range tanks.'

The story goes that Nichols had found a stockpile of Thunderbolt long range tanks and had commandeered a train destined for an Army Depot, and diverted it to Madras after loading his tanks onto it. I have no means of verifying this story and certainly did not enquire too closely into it at the time, but it was one of the many pieces of initiative which prompted me to recommend Nichols eventually for an OBE, which he received and richly deserved. On 15 July the three tonners returned with the tanks, all brand new in their wooden crates. Some were needed immediately to replace leaking and damaged ones in the squadrons while the remainder subsequently moved with the Wing when it left Ulunderpet.

The two squadrons at Tanjore were getting their share of the flow of replacement equipment and had settled down very well on a station which seemed to me to be more civilised than

Ulunderpet. It was less dispersed and had the advantage of quite a large village in the vicinity. Flying the 50 odd miles which separated us became a routine several times a week, sometimes in a Harvard and sometimes in a Thunderbolt.

A walk round Tanjore village was interesting as it was the centre of some attractive brassware known as 'Tanjore work'. I bought two large plates for some ridiculous amount like 10 Rupees. They were beautifully made, one being embossed with copper and Rupee silver, and the other engraved with inlaid copper and silver round the edge. These plates still give us pleasure more than forty years later and, unlike many Indian brass ornaments, I have never seen similar work for sale elsewhere.

I had one Chaplain in the Wing who had to look after both stations. He would conduct matins on a Sunday at Ulunderpet and then be flown down to Tanjore to hold an evening service. I flew him down myself on one Sunday afternoon in July and he arrived at the Harvard with a sack which he told me contained new hymn books. It was too bulky to fit into the small luggage locker, so he had to carry it on his lap. Before climbing into the rear cockpit he said, rather tentatively, 'Would you mind doing a slow roll on the way down?'

'I beg your pardon,' I said, looking at him in astonishment.

'You see, sir, it is considered in 904 Wing that hymn books are not operational until they have been slow rolled – and these are brand new.'

'Can you give me chapter and verse for that extraordinary custom?' I asked.

'No, sir, not specifically but (after a short pause and with a twinkle in his eye) the troops may feel it is a way of consecrating them.'

'Very well, but strap yourself in tightly and hang onto that sack or we may both be singing hymns elsewhere than at Tanjore.'

We took off and climbed to 5000 feet, away from the heat and dust.

'Ready?' I asked into my mouthpiece. A muffled sound came from the back which I took to be assent and dived gently down to reach 150 mph. Up with the nose and over to the right. I turned it into a bit of a barrel roll so that the padre wouldn't have to hang on his straps for too long, and out we came still pointing roughly towards Tanjore. I don't know how long it had been since that Harvard was last on its back, but the sand and dirt which came up from the floor was choking. Happily nothing more dangerous, like a couple of spanners, came with it. We landed and the padre pronounced the hymn books fully operational and fit for evensong. I was rather startled during the service when he announced that we had new hymn books and the Commanding Officer had kindly rolled them on the flight down. A ripple of noise ran through the congregation which was the nearest thing to a cheer that I've ever heard in church.

The problem of finding enough recreation to fill the leisure time of the airmen was not an easy one to solve. Most of them were pretty whacked after a day's work in the heat and, knowing that we were unlikely to be on these two isolated stations for very long, they seemed reasonably happy to eat, drink and sleep. Nevertheless I sent two officers to reconnoitre the delights of Pondicherry, but that was disappointing. The airmen were hardly likely to be fascinated by somewhat dilapidated French colonial architecture; there were few, if any, pretty French girls, and such bars and restaurants as existed were hot and unattractive. Due to wartime conditions the shops had little of interest in them. However, it was a town and a few 'liberty' runs were arranged for those who wanted a change, but reports from early visitors were not encouraging.

One recreational highlight, if one can call it such, was a visit to the local gin factory. We were favoured with two makes of Indian gin – Carews and Haywards. The Haywards plant was not far from Ulunderpet and a visit there became quite popular. On going to see it myself, I wished I had not seen in too much detail how our gin was made. Perhaps that is unfair as our hosts were always most welcoming and hospitable. To my knowledge there were no cases of suffering from its effects.

An open air cinema was rigged up on a bare patch close to the Sergeants' mess. That was popular and free of charge. With a glass of Muree beer in the cool of the evening the benches in the cinema were well patronised with a good supply of films for which I believe Nichols was again largely responsible. Live entertainment, however, was not forthcoming: it was most unlikely that ENSA had ever heard of our remote stations, and nobody above directed their footsteps towards us.

By mid July I was beginning to get seriously concerned about our future and what was in store for 904 Wing. There was nothing I could tell the airmen beyond my belief that an operation to liberate Singapore was planned for sometime in September, no more than two months ahead. I flew up to Bangalore on several occasions but no firm dates were forthcoming. I was expected to have my Wing fully operational by the end of August and be prepared to move shortly thereafter.

Apart from confirming my own expectations, this told me nothing. However, a rumour was starting to circulate in the tents of power in 224 Group, namely, that the Americans had developed a new weapon of devastating power. It has to be remembered that the atomic bomb was one of the best kept secrets of the war and neither I nor any of my colleagues had ever heard of it. It was no more than the vaguest of rumours and there was no knowledge as to how, or indeed whether, it could be used to shorten the war. The Americans were gaining the upper hand in the Pacific and there was a general feeling of optimism that the war could not last much longer. Nevertheless it looked as though we would have to go into Malaya and fight our way down to Singapore. The role of 904 Wing would be to occupy certain airfields on the west coast of Malaya after their capture by the assault forces and give close support to the Army as it fought its way down the peninsular. Paddy Bandon could give me no more information and was himself daily expecting something firm from the Commander-in-Chief in Kandy about future operations. There was a great air of expectancy within the Group headquarters, and I caught the feeling of excitement among the staff although none of them knew what they were excited about. It was 19th July when I flew the Harvard back to Ulunderpet wondering whether I had learned anything of value to tell my own staff. By the time I landed I had made up my mind to tell everybody that we were almost certain to go to Malaya in September, and we must have the squadrons ready by the end of August.

During my talk with Paddy Bandon in his tent at Bangalore he had complained bitterly that he was unable to get a decent bath unless he went along to one of the hotels in the city. I thought about this on my way home and an idea came to me. I asked Bill Brown, the Engineer officer, to see me the following morning.

'Bill, could you make a bath out of an unserviceable long range tank?'

'Well, er . . . I suppose so, but don't you have a bath of sorts in your basha?'

'It's not for me, but for the AOC, who is having difficulty in keeping clean.' 'Ah well,' he said, 'we could have a try and there are plenty of old tanks – a bit narrow at the tail end, but he could always cross his legs – leave it to me.'

A few days later a splendid bath was brought into my office. A Thunderbolt tank had been cut in half lengthways with the filling orifice left as a drain hole complete with rubber plug. The sharp surround had been covered with rubber and pedestal feet attached to the bottom. 'How's that for the abandoned Earl?' asked Bill with some pride. 'Quite splendid, perhaps a bit small for a big man, but better than having to go to the local hotel. Doubtless an Air Vice-Marshal can find some way of disposing of the bath water in a tent.'

Two days later the bath was dispatched to Bangalore by a three tonner on a routine run, with the compliments of 904 wing. Nothing was heard for a few days until the AOC called a conference of all the commanders of his Wings for the unusual hour of 6pm one evening. I flew up, using a Thunderbolt on this occasion as I was getting more accustomed to the aircraft. The COs of the five Wings in 224 Group trooped into Paddy's tent at 6pm, and there he was, sitting in his new bath, covered in soap. 'Help yourselves to a whisky and make yourselves at home,' he said, carrying on with his ablutions. My colleagues were even more startled than I was until he said: 'This is to demonstrate the remarkable initiative of 904 Wing. A little tight around the hips but very good value, thank you, David.' After a short pause for towelling and dressing (when we all averted our eyes) Paddy sat down at his desk and we got on with the conference. It was little more than a recapitulation of where we all stood but I came away reasonably satisfied with the current state of our own re-equipment.

As July drew to a close the four squadron commanders all reported that their squadrons were as operational as they were ever likely to be in the time available, lacking a few things but nothing of vital importance. It had not been possible to provide any training in air firing or rocket firing. There were no firing ranges available and, apart from flying out to sea to test guns, there was little that could be done to keep the pilots' hands in. This was not, however, as serious a deficiency as it might sound. All the squadron pilots were thoroughly experienced on the Thunderbolt and we were fortunate to have no new pilots who would have needed training. Provided that we were not left kicking our heels after September, I felt that the high level of experience would see us through the next operation.

Nichols continued with his herculean task of getting equipment from every conceivable source and must have travelled thousands of miles around India crammed into the back of a Harvard – he was a very big man and not as young as most of us. I had signals from him as far away as Peshawar on the North West Frontier stating that various loads were on their way.

On 31st July the four squadron commanders came together for a conference in my office to review any deficiencies and decide how we should report our operational status to the Group headquarters. There was enthusiastic agreement to a proposal that we should get all the aircraft up together and carry out a formation flight over the Bangalore headquarters. Before having a good lunch to celebrate in the Mess with plenty of Carews gin but the inevitable chicken curry, I drafted a signal to the AOC: '904 Wing now operational. Will demonstrate at 1200 hours 3rd August.' A reply came the following day 'Await your demonstration with interest.'

It was decided that Neil Cameron would lead the formation and that Wing Commander Whitehead would fly in the Wing Thunderbolt as a reserve in case anybody fell out during the flight. I had some doubts as to whether the squadrons could get all eighty aircraft into the air, but they were quite confident. 'In any case,' as somebody said, 'I can't see the Group staff counting up to eighty in about one minute: they'll be mesmerised by the size of the formation.' Finally it was decided that the two Tanjore squadrons would join up at 5000 feet over Ulunderpet at 1120 hours.

I was determined to see this from the Group headquarters and so, early on the morning of the 3rd I flew the Harvard up to Bangalore and joined Paddy Bandon and his staff with no little trepidation, and plenty of leg pulling from the staff.

At two minutes to 12 o'clock a dull roar was heard to the east and as near to 12 o'clock as makes no difference, Neil Cameron led his squadron over the camp at 2000 feet, followed in succession by the other three squadrons. If the formation was not quite up to the standard of the Red Arrows, it was pretty good for such an unwieldy mass. Somebody beside me said, 'For God's sake, how many are there?' 'Surely you can count up to eighty,' I replied with some feeling of satisfaction. They were all there and I could see Whitehead's lone Thunderbolt way out to one side, keeping an eye on the formation.

'They will be coming back shortly,' I said to the AOC. 'Well,' he said, 'you've got them flying: are they fully equipped?' 'Frankly no: there are items of armament and signals equipment which we still need, but I think another couple of weeks should see the Wing at least as well placed as it was in the Arakan.'

It took a long time to turn a formation of that size round without losing cohesion but within a few minutes the dull roar was heard again, from the west this time. Three squadrons roared overhead at 1000 feet and I could hear some speculation as to whether the fourth had lost itself. As the noise died away, the fourth squadron could be seen approaching low down at 500 feet. It was the squadron which, in addition to its normal ground attack role, had a smoke producing role as well – a requirement to produce a blanket of smoke when the Army needed smoke cover to hide behind. As the aircraft reached the perimeter of the camp, dense smoke poured from their special canisters under the wings, laying a thick blanket over the headquarters. The smoke, which was stannic chloride, was harmless enough, but sufficient to drive the staff officers into their tents, coughing and spluttering. I felt that Paddy Bandon was a little uncertain about this piece of realism, but after wiping his eyes, he said, 'Well, I think you've made your point and I must accept that 904 Wing is now operational, which makes three out of my five Wings.' Some of his staff were not quite so charitable, but the smoke drifted away very quickly and good humour was restored. One or two of my old friends like Bernard Chacksfield and Denis David even stood me a lunchtime drink, probably wishing they were commanding Wings and not pushing pens in tents.

I flew back to Ulunderpet feeling that we had just about 'got away' with our demonstration, but it could have gone wrong in other circumstances. A signal of congratulations went out to the four squadrons to which Neil Cameron replied and said 'Please don't ever ask me to turn round a formation of eighty aircraft again: it took all of fifty miles.'

Unbeknown to me, Neil had kept the formation together and flown over Ulunderpet for the benefit of the airmen who had worked so hard to get the Thunderbolts ready, and then completed a wide circle and flown over Tanjore before its two squadrons broke away and landed. I think every airman on both stations had turned out to see the sight and must have felt that their hard work was paying dividends.

We were now into August but the hot weather showed no signs of relenting and we were too far south and west to get much of the monsoon which, in this month usually brought torrential rain to north east India and Burma. On balance I think I preferred the heat to the appalling humidity which always accompanied the monsoon.

It was also getting close to the expected date for the operation to liberate Malaya and Singapore, but still no news was available and clearly we had to expect very short notice if it was to be laid on in September. In the meantime there was still much to do, particularly in kitting out the troops, assembling medical supplies and ensuring that all our vehicles were thoroughly reliable and waterproofed against the need to land over beaches. There was, indeed, much to do and not much time in which to do it.

4

Ready for Anything

A few days after our formation demonstration over Bangalore, a rumour, which hardened into news, spread through the station to the effect that an immense bomb had been dropped on a Japanese city from an American Super Fortress (B 29). On hearing this, I immediately rang up Group headquarters and was told, 'Yes, quite correct: an atomic bomb has been dropped on the city of Hiroshima. It has devastated some four square miles of the city centre and caused an estimated 78,000 casualties.'

This was staggering news – one bomb dropped by a single aircraft had created all that devastation. What was an atomic bomb? One had, of course, heard that clever scientists had been endeavouring to split the atom, but to be able to harness the power released into a single bomb was unbelievable. It certainly lent credence to the rumours heard earlier that the Americans were in process of developing a weapon of mass destruction.

I called George Rumsey in from the next office and told him the story. His reaction was similar to mine. 'If there are many more of those about', he said, 'the Japs can't possibly hold out and the war is likely to come to an end very soon.' It was obvious that the news had gone round the world and there was no need for us to observe any secrecy so I decided that we must tell the airmen as soon as possible. I asked George to assemble them in the dining room immediately after lunch and I would tell them all we knew. 'Then I will fly down to Tanjore and give a repeat performance,' I said.

I felt a great sense of inadequacy as the buzz of conversation died down on my entering the long, palm thatched dining room. I could only tell the airmen the sparse facts that I had, and there was bound to be a barrage of questions which I could not answer. I couldn't even tell them what an atomic bomb was, never having heard of it until that morning. Our ignorance emphasised the isolation of our position in the centre of India. Had I still been in my previous job as a planner in Whitehall, I would undoubtedly have acquired much more knowledge.

Perhaps the answer was to visit Bangalore the following day to see what could be gleaned from the gossip. The Wing Thunderbolt took me to Yelahanka very quickly in the relative cool of the morning and I was in the headquarters within an hour. It was buzzing with speculation but no real information. Paddy Bandon had gone off to Mountbatten's headquarters at Kandy and had left a message that he would fly round his five Wings if he could elicit more information. With that I had to be content and set off back home (which I now found myself calling Ulunderpet).

Coming in to land I was suddenly ordered to overshoot and go round again – runway obstructed was given as the reason. It looked all right to me but I opened the throttle, pulled out to the right and flew along the runway at 400 feet. Nothing – until at the far end I spotted the white figure of a small goat sitting in the middle of the tarmac. A young boy was also visible standing on the side of the runway, obviously afraid to go on and collect his animal. By this time the firetender was tearing down the centre of the strip; the goat got up and bolted while the firetender's crew had stern words with the small herdsman. The voice of the controller came through my headphones, 'Do one more circuit, sir, while we ensure that all is clear. Sorry about that.' It was not easy for the controller in a makeshift and not very high tower to spot everything on the 2000 yards of concrete. After landing, the Fire Section Sergeant came out to me and said, 'I gave the boy back his goat, sir; he had lost control of it and was very upset.' 'I suppose you gave him some chocolate as well,' I said. 'How did you know that from up there, sir?' 'I didn't, but I know you; you were once a farmer, weren't you, Sergeant? That's OK, but don't make too much of a habit of it or they will all think that's the way to get a bar of chocolate.'

While still digesting the information about the atomic bomb, news came through three days later that a second huge bomb had been dropped; this time on the city of Nagasaki. First reports indicated that the area devastated and, therefore, the casualties inflicted were of the same order as those produced by the Hiroshima bomb. 'Surely this can't continue,' everybody said. 'How many of these weapons do the Americans have, for Heaven's sake?'

None of our questions could be answered: we could only speculate. We did not have long to wait.

A few days later, on 14th August, Japan capitulated, and so, in the space of less than two weeks, we had moved from the prospect of a continuing long drawn-out struggle to a sudden end to the conflict. The news reached me by telephone from Paddy Bandon who said, 'I want you and the other Commanding Officers to fly up here immediately – before lunch, if possible, so that I can discuss future plans. But see that all your troops know of this splendid news before you take off.' Well, it didn't take long for the news to spread like wildfire round the station, and there was just time to telephone Tanjore before jumping into a Harvard.

Although capitulation following the two atomic bombs was not entirely unexpected, the suddenness of it took everybody by surprise. The assembly of shipping in the east coast ports, and even some of the loading for the Malayan operation had already started and was occupying the attention of staffs and planners at all levels. Understandably little had so far been done to consider what immediate steps would be taken when peace broke out.

Another serious problem now arose and was outlined to us by the AOC at this important conference. The Supreme Allied Commander, Lord Mountbatten, had arrived back at his headquarters in Kandy from a visit to London only the day before the capitulation with a new directive in his pocket which greatly extended the area of his command. Whereas it had comprised India and Ceylon, Burma, Siam, Malaya and Sumatra, his new directive involved taking over responsibility also for Borneo, Java, the Celebes and that part of Indo-China lying below the 16th Parallel. This increased his area from about one million to about one and a half million square miles. The additional area had been transferred from General MacArthur's American command in the South West Pacific, and the new directive was to take effect from the surrender of Japan which, at the time of issuing the directive, was not expected to be as early as 14th August.

Mountbatten's command now contained some 128 million people, among which were no less than 750,000 Japanese of whom 630,000 were armed troops. Of even greater importance, there was thought to be 123,000 Allied prisoners of war and internees scattered in camps throughout the theatre. Furthermore no reliable civil police force existed and, apart from Siam, there was no civil government which had even the shadow of an independent administration.

It was not surprising, therefore, that, with the sudden and unexpected end to hostilities and the enlargement of SEAC with so little warning, no plans for the immediate post-war occupation of the area existed at Kandy.

I flew quickly back to Ulunderpet from the conference to find my station in an uproar. Celebrations were in full swing in every mess and basha. 'The war is over and now we can all go home.' – But wait a minute; that was the second time I had heard that joyful exclamation in less than four months, first on VE day and now on VJ day. Although it 'appeared' that there was no more fighting to be done, it was very clear to me from the Bangalore conference which I had just left that an immense task remained and there could be no relaxation for the thousands of airmen in the Command.

Still, the first thing to do was to celebrate the victory and think about the future later. Following the well known tradition of British schoolmasters on suitable occasions, I declared the following day to be a holiday and instructed the officers to organize a sports programme followed by a firework display using any surplus pyrotechnics which were available. I reckoned that our armament section could be relied upon to come up with something spectacular. Although no work was to be done on aircraft, Neil Cameron asked if one Thunderbolt could give a 'victory' aerobatic display followed by a height judging competition for which the troops could buy tickets at one Rupee each.

My recollection of that momentous day off is somewhat hazy, but I do still have a photograph of myself coaching the Wing headquarters tug of war team to victory after a hard fought battle with the airmen of 131 Squadron. Cries of 'fiddle' were heard all round as the Group Captain's team took the prize of twelve bottles of beer. The aerobatic display by Flying Officer Denison of 258 Squadron was immaculate and, I was pleased to see, absolutely safe. I don't know how he arranged it but Denison managed to drop a large bag of flour from a bomb rack which burst suitably in the air and covered us all with a fine coating of flour. For the height judging competition, he flew over twice, in opposite directions, at 6200 feet, so he said;

and nobody could dispute his accuracy. Most of the Wing handed in their estimates to a panel of judges, the winner being a Corporal who got within 50 feet of the correct height, collecting a prize of 200 Rupees. I might add that he did not belong to 258 Squadron.

As darkness fell, the firework display began. It was hardly up to Crystal Palace standards but not a bad effort for a team of armourers who had only a few hours and very little material with which to mount one. Unfortunately it finished in disaster. A badly aimed green Very light fell onto the roof of the Sergeants' Mess. As palm leaf thatch is reputed to burn at 30 feet per minute, the building was reduced to ashes before the Fire Section could get into action. The only comforting aspect was that the building did not contain the NCOs' quarters and their personal belongings were not affected. The junior airmen were quick to spot that the offending cartridge had been fired by a Sergeant, and regarded it as fitting justice that it should fall on his own Mess.

Back in the isolation of my lonely basha I spent a fitful night and was worried. Several airmen had asked me during the day whether they would now be going home as the war was over. Some – the longer serving ones – probably would, but most of them clearly would not, with the task of clearing up the huge area of South East Asia to be tackled. However, with commendable speed, 224 Group was able to issue some general guidance and instructions within a few days. The first and vital task was to go to the aid of our prisoners of war scattered throughout the theatre. Because Japan had never fully complied with the Geneva Convention (which laid upon all nations the responsibility for publishing their POW camps), we had incomplete knowledge of the whereabouts of our prisoners. Over the years, Intelligence staffs had pieced together some locations but more were needed. Nevertheless a start could be, and was made immediately under the direction of a new organisation entitled RAPWI (Repatriation of Allied Prisoners of War and Internees).

Leaflets were to be dropped over all known camps, instructing the inmates to remain in situ, followed by airdrops of food and medical supplies. In addition, surrendered Japanese officers were interrogated in an attempt to find the location of any unknown camps. The next priority task was to get into the various countries, reach the camps and liberate the prisoners who were known to have suffered grievously during the past years.

It was obviously going to be a formidable humanitarian operation. We had a reasonably complete picture of the disposition of prisoners in Burma, Siam and Indo-China, but very little was known about the conditions in the more distant areas such as Malaya, Singapore, Sumatra and Java. What was to be the role of 904 Wing in all this, I wondered? The Thunderbolt could not be used to drop supplies and the distribution of leaflets was not really practicable. They could, however, be used to range far and wide in an endeavour to locate camps on the instructions of RAPWI, but clearly not from Ulunderpet or Tanjore.

I did not have long to wait. Part of the 224 Group force which had been limbering up to recapture Malaya and Singapore was to carry on with the projected operation and, as the assault fleet was already loading in the East coast ports, it was to land over the beaches in Malaya with, of course, no opposition, and re-occupy the Malayan peninsular and move down to Singapore. This was considered to be the quickest way to reach those particular areas, but the forces needed would not be as large as originally planned.

I then learned that my Wing would probably be reconstituted and go to the Netherlands East Indies, specifically to Java. This news came as something of a shock. My sketchy knowledge of Java told me that it was a large island in the NEI beyond Singapore, but other than that I knew nothing about it at all. It appeared that the whole of 224 Group was to be split up and various elements of it would move with all speed to the various parts of South East Asia where Japanese forces had to be disarmed and prisoners of war and internees rehabilitated.

Two questions immediately sprang to mind. What was the situation in Java and what would be the make-up of 904 Wing? It was quite clear that four Thunderbolt squadrons would not be a suitable force to liberate thousands of Allied prisoners. I must have more information before presenting my officers and airmen with a half baked story, and so I set off once again for Bangalore.

The Group was in turmoil with much midnight oil being burned in every office tent. All I could discover was that I was to pack up my Wing, retaining all its mobile equipment and move to Madras as soon as possible. 60 Squadron, historically the oldest squadron, was to remain with me but the other three would probably be disbanded in the near future. I would be joined at Madras, probably by one more Thunderbolt squadron from another Wing together with two squadrons of the RAF Regiment and a host of other mainly administrative elements. A transport squadron of Dakotas would be likely to join the Wing in Java and any other units which could help with the repatriation task. Nothing was known about the situation in Java but a small reconnaissance force was being dropped in Batavia by RAPWI, and a British Army contingent would go in as quickly as possible. With this sketchy information I had to be content, and knuckle down to the job. That was the last I saw of Paddy Bandon and his staff as they all expected to be going to Malaya – over the beaches and on to Singapore in accordance with the original operation.

The first task was to give the officers and airmen all the information I could and, for two days, I talked ceaselessly to all of them both at Ulunderpet and Tanjore. What I had to say met with a mixed reception as was to be expected and I played heavily upon our responsibility to rescue all those unfortunates who had fallen into Japanese hands, many of them since the fall of Singapore. We knew from reports on conditions during the construction of the Burma/Siam railway that many had suffered terrible privations and hundreds had died in captivity. There was some muttering and grumbling during my talks, but, in

41

general, the men accepted the news and felt that at least many old friends would be staying together.

A comprehensive repatriation scheme did exist, based upon the length of time individuals had served in South East Asia, but such was the scarcity of shipping due to wartime losses, and so few transport aircraft could be spared, that it was clear that repatriation would be a slow business, even for the highest priority men and women.

I received instructions to sort out my officers and airmen, taking to Java only those who were in fairly low categories for release. It was a difficult and not very palatable task but my staff tackled it in a few days. The list of those to be left behind disappointed me and included some of my best tradesmen and senior NCOs. Flight Lieutenant Nichols, who had been primarily responsible for equipping us so efficiently was on that list and I knew that his loss would be a particular blow. Had he been allowed to do so, I believe he would have volunteered to come to Java, but he had served since the beginning of the war and had a business awaiting his return to London.

The last two weeks of August and the early part of September were fully occupied with these tasks of sorting out personnel. It was decreed that the tour in South East Asia should be set at three years and four months. Everybody beyond that duration of tour was to be repatriated when transportation could be made available. Our other task was to ensure that the Wing was fully self-supporting in every respect as we had no idea what lay in store for us in Java. Vehicles for every purpose from firetenders to refuellers, tentage, clothing, rations, communications equipment, medical supplies and firearms were but a few of the categories of equipment required to make the Wing fully mobile. We were clearly going to be on our own and could not rely on support from elsewhere, at least in the early stages of the occupation.

I wondered what airfield we would take over. Would it be suitable for the Thunderbolt, which was quite a demanding aircraft when it came to runway lengths and strengths? Nobody could answer that question. Who would be my new boss? I knew that it would not be Paddy Bandon as he was destined for Singapore. Again, no answer: get on with the move and be prepared for anything.

As August came to an end, there were slight signs of a reduction in temperatures, particularly in the daytime. 90° seemed almost a relief after the 100° temperatures which had dominated the last two months. By 1st September, the Wing was ready to move and we felt ourselves to be reasonably self-supporting. Food was something of a problem, having no idea what lay ahead, and so we built up vast stocks of 'Compo' rations, unattractive and unappetising as they were, but at least we could survive on them until something better cropped up. Tinned M and V (meat and vegetables), self heating cans of soup and tinned cheese were part of the contents of these 'Compo' packs.

News now reached me that my second Thunderbolt squadron would be No 81 Squadron, under the command of Squadron Leader Pat Kennedy, a thoroughly experienced and seasoned unit which had fought its way through the Burma campaign. Pat Kennedy flew down to meet 904 Wing from his station further north, and I was happy that at least my two fighter squadrons would be compatible, having known each other in Arakan.

At last, early in September, some information about the situation in Java filtered through. It appeared that RAPWI had sent a team of Intelligence officers to be parachuted into Java and their initial report was, to say the least, disquieting. Apparently the Japanese forces there had realized a short time before the capitulation that their situation was hopeless and had persuaded the Indonesians to set up a government before any Allied forces could get there with a view to safeguarding the East Indies for their previous colonial masters, the Dutch. The Japanese were now, it was reported, handing over their arms to the Indonesians and sitting back, with smiles on their inscrutable faces, to await the arrival of the 'liberators'. The

43

RAPWI team said that a fair degree of chaos reigned and it was having the greatest difficulty in identifying the areas and camps where prisoners of war and internees were being held. The team was not being molested or threatened but, on the other hand, was receiving little or no co-operation from the new and hastily formed government.

It was clearly important that Mountbatten's forces reached Java with the minimum of delay in the hope of stabilizing the situation and extracting the Allied captives, who were mostly British, Australian and, of course, many Dutch. Within a few hours of receiving this news, I was instructed to move the Wing by road to Madras where some of the shipping previously concentrated for the Malayan operation would be allocated to me. I had not been given and, in fact, never did receive any written orders to go to Java, which gives some idea of the complications and the confusion which reigned after the unexpected and sudden collapse of the Japanese.

The Thunderbolt squadrons were ordered to fly north, mostly round into Burma where they could wait to be called forward by the SEAC forces in each of the countries to be occupied. I said farewell to my four squadrons with regret, knowing that 60 Squadron was the only one of them destined to join the Wing again in Java.

The remnants of the Wing concentrated at Ulunderpet and a few days later set off for Madras in several large convoys. Somewhere in the middle of this mass of transport George Rumsey and I travelled in the old Ford V8 staff car. Less than half way to Madras it broke its back axle and stranded us. Nobody was at all surprised, least of all myself. It was a dreadful old banger which should have been scrapped much earlier but it had proved impossible to get a replacement. We were picked up by the following troops and we transferred to a Jeep while the Ford was taken in tow by a three tonner. A good start, I thought, to a journey which looked like having many unknown hazards.

Madras was eventually reached and George and I made for the Madras Club as being the most likely place where we could get information. Sure enough we found a small harassed Movements staff endeavouring to sort out all the units and bodies of troops converging on the city from every direction. The harbour was crammed with military shipping and the city, a pleasant enough place at most times, was now a seething mass of soldiers and airmen, all destined for different parts of South East Asia.

George went off in our jeep to guide the 904 Wing airmen into a tented transit camp while I discovered that we had been allocated three ships in which we were to embark on the following day. It was a profitable evening as the commanding officers of two RAF Regiment squadrons and a unit of Air Formation Signals, as well as the Squadron Leader commanding a RAF Servicing Commando, found me and introduced themselves as new reinforcements for 904 Wing. A little order was beginning to emerge from the chaos and we cooked up a plan for getting our men aboard the ships the next day.

'Do you know where we are going?' asked the Regiment Wing Commander. 'I've been told the Wing is to go to Java,' I replied, 'but I've had no written instructions.' 'Yes, that has been the rumour reaching us, but the only orders I have had were to report to 904 Wing here.' The other units were in the same position, and so we decided over our beer that evening to embark our men, vehicles and stores and hope that more definite instructions would arrive. They did not.

Early the following morning I drove my jeep down to the docks to look at the fleet of three ships allocated to 904 Wing. That provided the next shock. I had been told that the main troop carrying vessel was a Landing Ship Infantry (Large), LSI(L) in military parlance. I had visualised some sort of landing craft, never having seen a LSI(L) before. To my amazement she was an ocean liner, the *Llanstephan Castle*, an ex-Union Castle ship of, as I learned later, 11,299 tons, built in 1914 and converted for wartime use with Landing Craft Assault (LCA) hanging round her davits in place of the lifeboats. She was manned by the Royal Indian Naval Reserve and, despite long service in South East Asia, she looked smart and impressive. The other two ships to carry our vehicles and heavy equipment were considerably smaller cargo carriers, able to take the few troops needed to look after our stores.

I went aboard to meet the captain of the *Llanstephen Castle*, an imposing and obviously senior skipper who, like his crew, was in the RINR but had been a Union Castle master in peacetime. He made me most welcome and we were soon on Christian name terms although he could not have been far short of twice my age. He gave me a great feeling of confidence. Despite being only breakfast time, we repaired to his cabin for a gin (Gordons, not Carews) while we tried to sort out the future.

'What are your instructions, David?' he asked. 'I've only had a verbal message that the Wing will go to Java, and that I am to bring it to Madras as quickly as possible where other units will join me.' 'Well,' said Bill, 'I have been told I am to take the RAF to Batavia and, furthermore, that I am to leave this berth within the next 48 hours as it is needed urgently for other shipping.' That seemed to settle matters and we decided there and then to set off as soon as our three ships were loaded. At that point the skipper threw in something of a bombshell. 'I also have strict orders,' he said, 'to maintain wireless silence throughout the voyage. This is because there may still be some Jap submarines lurking in the Indian Ocean who may not have received the cease-fire order. I think this is unlikely, but those are my orders.'

'That means,' I said, 'that we will have no means of finding out the situation in Java before we arrive. That could be extremely awkward, but I cannot believe the RAF would be committed to a dangerous situation at this stage, after the war is over. I assume that Headquarters at Kandy could send a one way message to you if such a situation arose.' 'We will maintain a listening watch at all times,' replied Bill, 'but, of course, even an incoming signal ought to be acknowledged and wireless silence would have been broken if only for a moment or two.'

'However,' said Bill, sensing a fairly worried Group Captain in front of him, 'Don't fuss too much about it: I have been to

46

Batavia before, in peacetime of course, and I know the docks at Tandjoeng Priok. We will approach cautiously, anchoring off if necessary, and hope to get some indication of what is happening ashore.'

With that encouragement, and with a second gin inside me, I went ashore to see how the loading was going. The quayside was a hive of activity. Vehicles were being swung aboard the two smaller ships and the airmen were filing into the *LLanstephan Castle* and being allocated their accommodation. I was watching a 15 ton firetender being hoisted aloft when, to my horror, the lifting cables snapped and the vehicle fell with an appalling crash onto the dock side. Its wheels splayed out and it came to rest at a drunken angle. By a miracle nobody was underneath it. It produced a roar of cheers from the troops, but it didn't amuse me as it was our biggest and best fire fighting vehicle – apparently a complete write off. Nevertheless it was hoisted aboard and the transport section eventually managed to repair it in Java.

By nightfall all the officers and airmen were aboard and more comfortably accommodated than I expected. Some vehicles and stores remained to be loaded but the work went on throughout the night under the very efficient supervision of the Indian crews, so that by 10 o'clock on the following morning, we were ready to sail.

As I still had received no written orders, and now having no Group Headquarters to refer to, I sent a signal to the Command Headquarters in Kandy, stating that 904 Wing was leaving for Java and, in view of the need to maintain wireless silence during the voyage, I would expect instructions to reach me in Batavia.

47

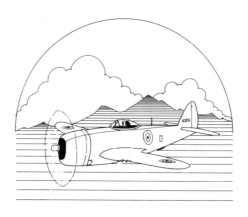

5

The Voyage

It was a brilliant late September morning when we steamed slowly out of Madras harbour, closely followed by the two stores ships. I had a permanent invitation to be on the bridge whenever I liked and also to accompany Bill on his daily Captain's rounds of the ship. As soon as we were well out to sea, George Rumsey and I decided to tour the ship, talk to the troops and inspect their accommodation.

The *Llanstephan Castle* was a grand old lady, built by Scottish shipbuilders in 1914 for the luxury trade to South Africa. The pre-war furniture and many fittings had been removed for her war service, but she retained much of the old mahogany panelling, staircases and also the decorative work on ceilings and walls. Big areas had been cleared for troop decks with rows of bunks and excellent toilet facilities. In general the

48

men were much more comfortable than they had been at Ulunderpet and, doubtless, at the other stations in India from which many had come. The ship was well supplied with food, beer and cigarettes and, if only we had known what lay in store for us at the other end, the voyage could have been almost a pleasure cruise. The crew rigged up huge canvas ventilators which pumped air into the ship as soon as she was under way. Conditions were not at all bad, but it would obviously get hotter and hotter as we approached the Equator.

The composition of the Wing had changed dramatically with the influx of new units, but it was a comfort to find that many of the NCOs were long service regulars who were not as unhappy at 'continuing the war' as some of the hostilities-only airmen. Nevertheless, the many groups scattered around the spacious decks – Regiment airmen, soldiers of Air Formation Signals and Servicing Commando men were getting to know each other and swapping impossible yarns of their experiences.

'George,' I said, as we returned to my cabin-cum-office after two hours of circulating round the ship, 'have we any idea of the new strength of the Wing? It was about one thousand at Ulunderpet and Tanjore'.

He thought for a while. 'Not a very accurate assessment until we get everybody together, but talking to the various unit commanders and guessing at those units still waiting to join from Burma, my guess is that the Wing will be much bigger, and could be as large as 2600 men all told.' In due course it turned out that his estimate was very accurate.

The next few days of glorious but hot weather were busy. Lifeboat drill and the allocation of the men to the Landing Craft (Assault) – LCAs – which did duty as lifeboats, was important in view of the slight possibility of attack. The LCAs were not, of course, equipped like unsinkable lifeboats. They had good engines but lacked seats and stocks of food although we put iron rations and water aboard each one. There was, however, plenty of space for everybody on board the ship but, designed as they were to carry assault troops a short distance from ship to beaches, LCAs were not particularly seaworthy and would probably not survive for long in a heavy sea. However, augmented with life rafts, they were all we had, and so every man was allotted his craft and mustered with lifejackets twice in the first few days, organised by my new OC Flying, Wing Commander Ted Cotton, who had joined the Wing at Madras. He was a cheerful extrovert who soon made himself popular with the airmen, taking a lot of responsibility off my shoulders.

On the fourth day out, George Rumsey came to me and said, 'We've left one important item behind. There is no RAF ensign among our equipment to hoist on our new airfield. We had only one, and we left it with the remnants of the Wing at Ulunderpet.'

This was a problem. I didn't fancy having to lower a Japanese flag and be unable to replace it with our own. 'What about a Union Jack, George?' 'No', he said. 'We have never possessed one, but I suppose the ship might be able to produce one.'

Somebody, and I don't remember who it was, had an idea. There existed at the time, a useful little book of general RAF knowledge known as the RAF Pocket Book. It contained the details and dimensions of the RAF ensign, so the thought was born that perhaps we could make one.

We took the problem to the Captain. 'Well,' said Bill, 'let's see what my Yeoman of Signals can find in the way of suitable bunting: we have masses of flags in the signals locker.' The Yeoman of Signals, an Indian Chief Petty Officer, could not have been more helpful. He turned out his locker and produced various pieces of bunting of different colours. Red, white and blue for the roundels posed no problem but the pale blue of the RAF was more difficult. The nearest we could get was a light blue which was several shades darker than the official colour.

'What about the small Union Jack to go in the top corner?' I said. 'We can cut one from an old Red Duster.' (The Merchant Navy ensign), replied the Yeoman.

The troops were vastly intrigued as, with the Pocket Book in one hand and a tape measure, we chalked out the dimensions of

50

the flag on the boat deck. The size had to accord with the dimensions of the small Union Jack which was brought along by the Yeoman, and then the cutting out could start.

'I'll have to sew on the roundels and the Jack, but I have a sewing machine; the trickiest part will be to make perfect circles of red, white and blue, but I'll do my best.' The Yeoman had entered into the spirit of the thing and was clearly delighted with this unusual chance to show his skill. He made an excellent job of it, and the next day the completed flag was spread out on our chalked pattern. I had to admit that it looked very peculiar, mainly because the pale blue was wrong but, nevertheless, it was a good effort and certainly the best that was possible. 'If you are satisfied with it,' said the Yeoman, 'I'll stitch the halyards and clips onto it and the captain has given me permission to hoist it for a test flight'.

Our small convoy ploughed on towards the Sunda Strait between Sumatra and Java where any risk of Japanese interference was considered to be greatest.

My Commanding Officers and I held a conference with the Captain to discuss what measures we should take to meet any possible situations when we approached Batavia. We knew that we could not expect to receive information about conditions there in view of the wireless silence. Would we have to carry out a landing on the Javanese beaches or would we have to make a ceremonial entry into Batavia? The first seemed highly unlikely and was obviously fraught with danger: the second was a possibility but one for which we were equipped, and which only the RAF Regiment could perform with adequate dignity.

The outcome of this discussion was that, before we reached the narrow passage of the Sunda Strait, the ship would heave-to for an hour or two, the LCAs would be lowered and manned by our RAF Regiment, armed and prepared to practise a beach landing. It would be a good exercise and would give the two Regiment squadrons a real purpose. The Captain thoroughly approved of this as the LCAs had not been launched for twelve months and it would give his crew some much needed experience and also confirm that the landing craft were fully serviceable.

The ship duly hove-to and the 600 Regiment airmen boarded their allotted LCAs fully armed and equipped. Both squadrons were Rifle squadrons as opposed to Anti-Aircraft squadrons. With a few minor hitches, all the LCAs were lowered and their engines started up. Under the Wing Commander's orders they formed up and simulated the arrival at a beach, opening fire with rifles and mortars appropriately. It was pretty unrealistic, but it did acquaint the airmen with the conditions in the landing craft which were completely foreign to them. An hour later they were all safely back on board and the voyage continued.

The second possibility of a ceremonial entry into Batavia seemed highly unlikely but, nevertheless, there could be some need for a parade of some kind and this was the opportunity to ensure that we could appear as smart as our operational kit would permit. RAF Regiment uniform and that of the Servicing Commando was still the jungle green from Burma. The remainder of the officers and airmen had a mixture of jungle green and khaki drill. Many of the new arrivals in the Wing had come with khaki as the RAF would gradually change back to its usual peacetime tropical dress. A parade was held on the boat deck and it soon became clear that the Regiment would have to provide the leading elements and bulk of any parade which might be required on arrival. With white belts and jungle green battledress, the men were the most presentable; indeed I felt that they were pretty smart and certainly well disciplined. I had reason then, and even more later to be grateful for this excellent addition to the Wing. I inspected them with their Wing Commander and left them in no doubt that they would be responsible for upholding the efficiency of the Wing if we had to participate in any ceremonial. Apart from some rifle practice against old oil drums thrown over the stern, those were about all the preparations we could make.

The ships were now approaching the Sunda Strait between Sumatra and Java through which we had to pass. It was a time of more tension as the narrow waters were ideal for any possible depredations by Japanese submarines but as it was now more than a month since the capitulation, we felt that the word must surely have reached all Japanese shipping. But there was always the faint chance of a 'rogue', and look-outs were doubled-up on the ships for the passage of the Strait.

It was an interesting passage because in the centre lay the island of Krakatau, a small volcanic hillock which had blown up many years earlier. So violent had been the eruption that a vast cloud of dust had been seen and felt at an immense distance from its source. We passed close to Krakatua and one could clearly see the volcano with a completely flat top, left when the summit had blown off. It was an astonishing sight and one of the ship's officers gave a most interesting description of the incident over the ship's public address system. Those who had cameras were snapping away all along the port side of the ship which temporarily developed quite a list.

Within a few hours the Sunda Strait was left behind without any sort of incident and the extra look-out precautions were relaxed. We now had to round the tip of Java and sail in towards Batavia. The ship's library and chart store contained quite a lot of material about the island and my officers and I read up all we could about its geography, population, etc. The country is rather more than 600 miles in length and about 150 miles wide in the centre, with a high volcanic backbone running most of its length. The astonishing statistic to me was that the population at that time was given as 51 million, one of the most densely populated areas of the world, almost all the inhabitants being concentrated in the coastal plains. The climate was said to alternate between extremely hot and very wet, which was to be expected of a tropical island so close to the equator, but fortunately the monsoon which starts in North East India and Burma and then moves south, tended to peter out before reaching the East Indies. That was some consolation as the stories I had heard of monsoon conditions in Burma were horrifying. Burma was alleged to have 300 inches of rain a year.

A long conference was held in the Captain's cabin with his senior officers and mine present to discuss how we should approach the Batavia harbour of Tandjoeng Priok, some five miles out from the city.

'There is almost certain to be a minefield protecting the inner harbour,' said Bill. 'We must certainly assume so anyway, and I intend to anchor about 20 miles out and take stock of the situation. We should reach that point tomorrow evening and I suggest that the three ships should anchor close together and one or two of our LCAs should circle the ships all night with your Regiment men on board as a precaution against the ad- mittedly unlikely event of limpet mines being stuck on our hulls. If nothing transpires by dawn next day, we will steam very slowly towards the harbour with the other ships in line astern and two LCAs ahead to watch for floating mines. I think, David, you should brief your troops on this plan and ensure that they remain fully alert and know their lifeboat drill. When we anchor tomorrow evening, I will get the Captains of the other two ships to come aboard to have our plan explained to them. Any questions?'

Bill had made a long speech and produced a thoroughly competent plan. Apart from a few questions of detail, nobody had much to say. That evening I briefed the men over the public address system and also told them as much as the reference books had told me about Java. They must have found it extra- ordinary that their officers were leading them into a situation without the faintest idea of what would transpire. Surely, I thought to myself, if the situation in Java is really dangerous, wireless silence will be broken and we will be stopped or turned back. With that not particularly comforting thought, I spent a somewhat troubled night.

As the sun was setting the following evening, we reached a point some 20 miles from Batavia but the heat haze was such that it was impossible to see the shoreline. The ship hove-to and a whole series of lamp signals were exchanged with the other ships, resulting in a tight little formation with the two smaller

54

ships close to the stern of the *Llanstephan Castle*. Two LCAs were manned, by both Indian naval personnel and several Regiment gunners with their rifles loaded. Throughout that night they slowly circled our three ships, changing crews at two hour intervals. Nothing was seen or heard and they were hoisted aboard at first light. It was a sweltering night with the ships stopped and all the troops dossed down on deck to get what little sleep they could. A most uncomfortable – indeed an anxious – night for everybody.

As soon as the landing craft were secured, the convoy moved slowly ahead and I joined Bill on the bridge. 'The next few hours should provide answers to some of your problems,' he said with his binoculars glued to his eyes. The troops were all on deck and standing at their lifeboat stations as a precaution against hitting a mine.

After an hour's slow steaming, a long, low grey shape gradually materialised out of the haze ahead. 'It's a warship and I think it's a destroyer,' said the Officer of the Watch. A few moments later, a signal lamp started winking from the warship and the gist of the message was that it was a British destroyer which wanted to know who we were and what we were carrying. A great sigh of relief ran round the bridge as the Yeoman of Signals was instructed to reply that we were the *Llanstephan Castle* carrying the Royal Air Force accompanied by two stores ships. We were then told to stop and await instructions.

A long pause of half an hour or more ensued, during which Ted Cotton stood down the troops for breakfast and announced the good news that we were not alone. The destroyer's lamp started to wink again with a long message which, when translated, informed us that she was guarding the port side of a swept channel through a minefield. The channel was half a mile wide and marked by buoys at intervals. We were to proceed slowly in line astern towards the entrance to the inner harbour. 'Beware of a sunken ship lying across the harbour entrance. Good luck', was the end of the message.

We moved in slowly past the destroyer when the customary naval compliments were paid, and two lines of buoys showed up clearly. Speed was kept down to five knots with our two ships following in our wake. The flat shoreline was now clearly visible as was the semicircular breakwater surrounding the inner harbour. A large merchant ship was lying on its side, most of its hull showing above water and blocking at least half of a narrow entrance. 'That will take some shifting,' commented Bill, 'but presumably there is no other obstruction or we would have been warned.' Maintaining as slow a speed as would retain steerage way, the ship eased past the wreck and we entered Tandjoeng Priok harbour at mid-day. It was 17th October, and the voyage was nearly over.

A scene of utter devastation met our eyes. It later transpired that a Japanese ammunition ship had blown up some months earlier and razed almost every building in the docks to the ground. There seemed to be no sign of life in what one would have expected to be a busy port. Most, if not all, of the cranes had been demolished and, although some effort had been made to clear the quays, they were still littered with rubble. However, a signal flashed from a tower at one end of the docks, telling us to berth alongside.

Bill selected what seemed to be the largest and least cluttered quay through his binoculars and, with great care and skill brought our ship alongside with space astern for the other ships. No help in docking was forthcoming but that did not seem to worry our crew who secured the ship to the bollards which were about the only things left standing. I was full of admiration for the manoeuvre but the crew appeared quite accustomed to it.

We had arrived in Java. What now? There was nobody to meet us and the few native workmen clearing away wreckage took not the slightest notice of our arrival. It was now four o'clock with no more than three hours of daylight left. A conference of the Commanding Officers was called in Bill's cabin after taking the precaution of posting armed sentries at the head of the gangway which had been lowered.

The only thing we knew, or at least surmised, was that there must be some British in the town in view of the presence of the destroyer and the swept channel through the minefield. There was no point in starting to unload until we had more knowledge of the conditions in Batavia: indeed it could be dangerous.

'As it's so late in the day,' I said, 'we must stay aboard tonight and, if nothing has happened by tomorrow morning, we will put a couple of our jeeps ashore, and I'll drive into the town with a Regiment guard.' That was agreed as the light began to fade, which was more than could be said of the heat which was intense. The lights on all three ships were left on with several sentries patrolling the docks and two on the dockside at the foot of the gangway with orders to challenge anybody who approached the ship.

'Well,' said Bill, as we all took a 'cooler' in his cabin, 'I've got you to Java safely, and the next move is up to you. You are welcome to stay aboard until your problems are sorted out. In fact, I shall be sorry to lose you all; it's been an interesting voyage, and I've had a few in recent years.'

With the troops lying about half naked on the decks in an effort to find any puff of breeze going, we spent another steamy and restless night wondering what the dawn would bring. The most unusual voyage of my life was over. The old *Llanstephan Castle* and her Indian crew had done us proud.

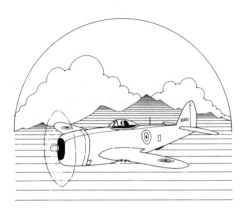

6

The Arrival

At dawn a faint breeze was moving our RIN ensign and giving a little relief to the airmen on deck after the sweltering, airless night. I was up on the bridge with Bill as the light grew and we surveyed the scene. Nothing moved except the dust which eddied out from the piles of debris in the puffs of wind. Our sentries and lookouts had seen and heard nothing all night. There were no other ships in our part of the docks but glimpses of a few masts could be seen in the distance. It rather looked as if we had berthed in the area of greatest devastation.

Bill and I continued our previous day's discussion and agreed that two jeeps should be swung ashore at once. At 9 o'clock George Rumsey and I, with a Regiment escort of six airmen would set off for the city, leaving Ted Cotton in command of the Wing remaining aboard. Fortunately our three ships were equipped with derricks capable of carrying out the unloading although it would obviously have been quicker with the help of dockside cranes. Those close to us were nothing more than heaps of twisted girders lying on the ground, and so we were thrown back on our own resources.

'You have most of the problems,' said Bill, 'but I have a small one of my own. As a visitor to a foreign port I should fly the flag of the host nation, but I don't know what it is. There is no Indonesian flag to my knowledge, or if there is, we certainly don't have one. I can't hoist the Dutch flag for obvious reasons, so what do I do?' He chuckled. 'It wouldn't be appropriate to fly your home made RAF flag, and in any case, you don't possess a spare. I've decided to hoist nothing.' 'Ah well, Bill, I can't take your problem too seriously: I have enough of my own at the moment. Meanwhile I'll have my last good breakfast.'

With much clanking of winches, the sailors extracted two jeeps from one of the holds and lowered them onto the dockside. A Sergeant and five Regiment airmen were detailed as escort and I held a short briefing session with them. We would travel slowly in company with rifles and revolvers loaded but hidden from view, and look for any signs of British life as I was convinced there must be some form of British authority in Batavia by this time.

As I walked out onto the deck, I could see a figure hurrying up the gangway. It was an officer in khaki drill wearing a braided RAF cap. As he approached he seemed familiar to me and I soon realised it was Group Captain Robert Sorel-Cameron, whom I knew slightly. Meeting him at the head of the gangway, I said as we shook hands, 'Thank God you've come. What on earth goes on here?' 'You may well ask; there's absolute chaos in the island – any chance of a decent breakfast?' By this time, Bill had come down from the bridge and was introduced as we made our way to the dining room.

As Sorel-Cameron, looking tired and drawn, tucked into a hearty breakfast, he began to explain the situation. 'We knew you were coming, but owing to the wireless silence, we had no idea when and no means of getting in touch with you.' 'You say "we knew you were coming", Sorel. Who do you mean by we?' I asked.

'Give me a chance and I'll explain,' gulping down half a cup of coffee. 'An Indonesian Government has been set up under a Dr Soekarno but, at the moment, it has control of little more than Batavia and its immediate surroundings. The Government is polite and reasonably friendly towards the British, realising that we have had to come in to disarm the Japanese, of whom there are about 26,000, and extricate prisoners of war and internees. Unfortunately there is suspicion among the Javanese population that we are here to hand their country back to the Dutch. The situation is extremely delicate and there is a great risk of troops being mistaken for Dutchmen.'

He then went on to say that a small Allied force under General Christison had arrived and set up a Headquarters in the city with Air Commodore Stevens who was organising an Air Headquarters of which he, Sorel-Cameron, was the Senior Officer in charge of Administration. I was breathing more and more sighs of relief, helped by cups of coffee, as this explanation continued. Bill, too, was looking increasingly cheerful as he could see the weight of the RAF being lifted from his shoulders.

Sorel-Cameron went on to tell us that, not only had the Japanese encouraged the Indonesians to set up a government before the Allies arrived, but had also handed over most of their weapons and trained some of the natives to use them. This had all started some three weeks before the capitulation when the Japanese realised that they could not win the war.

As a result of all this the British, as Sorel-Cameron put it, had become 'the meat in the sandwich.' The Dutch were mostly in prison camps and were hated by the Indonesians and the new government was highly suspicious of British intentions: it was not going to be easy to convince it that our presence was entirely humanitarian and designed only to return the Japanese forces to their own country and release the prisoners of war and internees.

'The AOC wishes you to take over the airfield at Kemajoran,'* said Sorel-Cameron. 'It was the peacetime Batavia airport on the edge of the city and at the moment the Japanese Air Force is still in occupation but, of course, disarmed. I'm afraid you'll get a shock when you see it: there is complete chaos there but it is the only possible airfield in the neighbourhood. We want you to get your squadrons in as quickly as possible. I suggest that you get the unloading under way at once, spend another night in the ship and move in convoys to the airfield tomorrow. In the meantime, I will do my best to arrange accommodation for your men which will not be easy as there is very little barrack accommodation on the airfield itself, bearing in mind that it was a civil airport before the war. A Japanese Brigadier is in command at the moment and your first task will be to take over from him. And that, David, is about all I can tell you at the moment.' There was little more to be said and, after a few more questions, most of which Sorel-Cameron could not answer, he hurried off down the gangway to sort out our accommodation.

Word had gone round and unloading had started even before the Group Captain had departed. It continued all day and throughout the night under the arc lamps of our ships. The lack of dockside cranes slowed the process down as some of the vehicles and items were almost beyond the capacity of the ship's derricks but by the following morning it was almost complete. The amount of equipment which the Wing possessed was staggering when seen on the devastated quays.

During the night we divided the Wing into about half a dozen small convoys, each led by a senior officer to avoid the whole contingent arriving at this unknown airfield in one large and unwieldy mass. They say that 'time spent in reconnaissance is seldom wasted', and I wanted time to carry out that preliminary survey before being inundated by over 2000 troops and a hundred or more vehicles.

'Don't rush it,' said Bill. 'You are welcome to let some of your

*Pronounced Kem-ire-on.

61

men spend another night in the ships if you meet with any major problems.' I was grateful for that offer but, in the event, we did not need to take advantage of it. 'My last request to you, Bill, is to ask you to give the troops a good breakfast as I'm pretty sure we will be on compo rations from then on.'

Early next morning I said goodbye to Bill and his crew and thanked them all for looking after us so well and so safely. My small convoy of six vehicles set off with the Regiment airmen smartly dressed and well armed against any eventuality but with their weapons hidden below the sides of the vehicles. The last thing we wanted to do was to create a hostile atmosphere. As we drove off, the old *Castle* gave a farewell blast on her siren and I looked back with some feeling of regret: she had provided the most comfortable quarters since leaving home six months earlier. I had also discovered a case of Gordons gin on the floor of my jeep, obviously a parting present from Bill whom unfortunately I never saw again. He had to return to Madras, doubtless to take more contingents to far away places. However, I discovered that he did take some of our prisoners of war who had been incarcerated in or near Batavia and were the first to be rescued.

We drove slowly on a long straight road through several small kampongs where the local Javanese looked at us with interest and seemed friendly. Like all Javanese they were neat and attractive people but there were not many smiling faces among them. The road to the city ran alongside a wide canal and the first thing one noticed was that it was filthy and sluggish, choked with weeds and floating debris. The air of neglect was all too evident which showed that the three years of Japanese occupation had done much to destroy the inherent neatness and cleanliness of the Dutch.

There was no need to go into the city as Kemajoran lay between it and the docks, up a side turning from the main road on which we were travelling. I stopped our convoy before reaching this turning and put my Group Captain's pennant on the jeep's flagstaff, also making sure that George Rumsey had our famous RAF flag.

'Now for it, George. I'll bet you've never started a new posting like this before. Sorel-Cameron said he would meet us at the airfield at 9.30 am with whatever arrangements he had been able to make about accommodation.' We drove slowly up the approach road and Sorel-Cameron was waiting at the gates with another Group Captain who turned out to be Hughie Edwards, the Senior Air Staff officer at our new headquarters. Edwards was a famous airman who had won the Victoria Cross in Bomber Command and who, in later years, was to become the Governor of Western Australia.

The first sight of Kemajoran was not inspiring. The camp appeared to consist of a pretty miserable collection of single storey buildings until we drove through onto the tarmac when an appalling sight met our gaze. There were dozens of Japanese aircraft, all wrecked and lying at drunken angles around the airfield, some on their bellies, some standing on their noses and others with one wheel retracted and sitting on a wing tip. 'Nasty sight, isn't it?' said Hughie, quite enjoying my exclamations of horror.

'Where are the Japanese?' I enquired. Sorel-Cameron then explained that Air Commodore Stevens had taken the surrender the previous day and instructed the Japanese airmen to build themselves a tented camp on the far side of the airfield. Until they could be repatriated they would be available to me as a labour force to get some sort of order out of the chaos.

The first thing to do was to hoist the RAF flag, and I had already noticed a tall flagstaff with two yard-arms standing between one of the small buildings and the tarmac apron. As we unfurled our flag Sorel-Cameron exclaimed, 'Good God, what is that?' 'That,' I said, 'is a genuine homemade RAF flag and unless you can produce a better one within fifteen minutes, it will have to do.'

My Regiment escort lined up in front of the flagstaff and their Sergeant attached the flag which he slowly hoisted onto the right hand yard-arm while we officers stood at the salute. It looked terrible but I was rather proud of it. Thus Royal Air Force Kemajoran came into being, the first and almost certainly the last time the RAF had an operational station in Java.

Hughie Edwards and I set off on a quick inspection of the airfield. There were two runways, each of 1600 yards in the shape of a 'V' with turning circles at each end. The surface was tarmac but badly cracked and broken in many places. The open ends of the 'V' were joined by the tarmac apron in front of the buildings, equally cracked and rutted. To the side of one runway was a flimsily built control tower, nothing more than a wooden cabin on stilts with access by a ladder.

'What do you think of this, Hughie?' 'Not much,' he replied. 'I'm sure these runways are too short for a Thunderbolt when fully loaded and the surface is terrible. I can imagine lumps of tarmac flying in all directions. They should be adequate for Dakotas and other less demanding aircraft. Anyway, it's all there is and you'll obviously have to operate the Thunderbolts with the greatest care and probably less than full load.'

The problem of parking 25 Dakotas, 40 Thunderbolts and probably a number of other aircraft was going to take some solving as only the grass area in between the runways was available and that would probably be unusable after the heavy rains which I understood we would get during the next few months.

Back to the tarmac apron to look at the three small buildings which had clearly been the civil administrative offices and two very small hangars, each of which might take half a dozen Thunderbolts but nothing larger, and certainly not Dakotas. Behind these buildings were a number of others including a palm thatched 'basha' type dining hall, some rudimentary kitchens but very little barrack accommodation. There was rubbish everywhere; water would not flow from anything more than two feet above ground level: no telephones and an extremely poor electricity supply.

It was a far from encouraging reconnaissance but, thank goodness we were a self contained mobile Wing and I knew that we could provide most of the important facilities from our own resources. The first essential was to get the airmen accommodated.

Sorel-Cameron had worked wonders. He had requisitioned a whole street of detached houses close to the station which I guessed had been used by the Japanese. As the convoys began to arrive at intervals of an hour, they were directed by my staff to these houses at least for the first night with a view to sorting them out later. Some of the overflow had to bed down in the hangars and administrative buildings for that night which was not too uncomfortable on a fairly cool, fine night. The Officers' Mess turned out to be a small hotel back on the main road which had also been used by the Japanese. It was a single storey building with a wide verandah in front, a long passage down the centre with about twelve rooms opening off it and a dining room with a kitchen at the rear. By doubling up in most rooms it housed all the Wing headquarters officers.

By nightfall all the troops had arrived and were settling in with much cheerful grumbling. As my Warrant Officer pointed out 'it's when an airman doesn't grumble something is seriously wrong and needs looking into at once.' Very wise words from one who should know!

That evening after an appalling supper of 'compo' rations, I opened Bill's case of gin and called a meeting to discuss plans for the following day. All my staff drew their chairs round in a semi-circle on the big verandah of our new home and, with each charged with a glass of gin, we started.

'We have to clear away the wreckage and bring the Thunderbolts in just as soon as we can. That is number one priority', I said, opening the discussion. This was to be Ted Cotton's job as Wing Commander Flying. It was agreed that he should have as many airmen and Japanese labour as he needed with all the resources of the transport section with regard to lifting gear and vehicles.

'The Japanese have made this mess, so see that they clear most of it away to the far side of the airfield, sweep the runways and choose the best of the two for the Thunderbolts to land on.'

Air Traffic Controllers and the Air Formation Signals contingent were then told to get at least radio communication working in the flimsy tower, and see what they could do to install the more important telephone lines: we had noticed that most of the phones had been ripped out but much of the wiring seemed to be in place and Air Formation Signals were experts at this job.

'George, I think you must concentrate on getting the airmen settled in as comfortably as possible, organise the messing arrangements and see what are the prospects for fresh fruit and vegetables. The country looks very lush and one would imagine that tropical fruits grow in profusion.

'New security. As far as I could see there is no perimeter fence and the airfield is open to every thieving rascal who wants to come in. So the first job for the Regiment must be to arrange guard posts, sentries and protection for our more valuable equipment stocks. In view of the political situation, all sentries must, of course, be armed with one up the spout at all times and be meticulous about challenging strangers. In due course we will arrange some form of pass system but, in the meantime, treat everyone with the utmost suspicion.' There were many more facilities to be provided – a transport yard, workshops, a medical centre to name but a few – but it was an experienced Wing and every section head knew what he had to do and I was happy to let them get on with it. Our first meeting ended with another gin as we dispersed for our first night in Java, a hot sultry night in our stuffy and rather smelly hotel. I made a mental note that hygiene might well be a problem, as indeed it turned out to be.

It was an early start next morning as I had decided that we would work our Indian routine in view of the heat: namely, a 6 am start with breakfast at 8 o'clock and then on until 1 pm. Work would probably be necessary in the afternoon, but I felt that we should wait and see what the conditions and the climate turned out to be before making a firm decision. As I reached my new and still very scruffy office, the Orderly Sergeant was raising the colour on the flagstaff outside the office window. Sorel-Cameron was calling for me at 6.30 am to take me into town to meet my new AOC and, hopefully, General Christison.

66

Before that, however, my driver Corporal Pattison came to see me saying, 'I have a pleasant surprise for you, sir. I have found a fine Buick Straight Eight sedan. It's only about three years old and in very nice condition, complete with a flagstaff and,' he added as an afterthought, 'a Japanese pennant in the dashboard locker.' That certainly was the best piece of news since arriving. Apparently quite a collection of vehicles had been left by the Japanese and it was possible to make use of some of them but the Buick, which had certainly belonged to the Japanese commanding officer, was the pick of the bunch. I think it had undoubtedly been a civilian vehicle commandeered by our predecessors.

I had never met Air Commodore Stevens and he welcomed me warmly, saying how relieved he was that we had arrived, as the General had plans which would most certainly involve the RAF fully. He then collected Hughie Edwards and Sorel-Cameron and we went along the passage to see the General and to hear his immediate plans.

Lieutenant General Sir Philip Christison had come straight from commanding a Corps in Burma and he was very well versed in the value of air support, with a particular knowledge of the work of Dakotas and Thunderbolts in the theatre. He walked over to a map of the island. 'This small area around Batavia is the only part of the island over which this new government has effective control and so at the moment it is our only British bridgehead, being held by my 23 Division. Consequently,' he continued, 'it is the only place where we can release the prisoners, and most of those in Batavia are women who have been separated from husbands on whose whereabouts we have little information.'

The General went on to say that he had a small RAPWI cell on his staff and they were trying to piece together from the government exactly where the prisoners were being held. It was already pretty clear that most of them were in various camps in the interior and were going to be very difficult to reach in the hostile atmosphere which prevailed. 'I have elements of 5 (Indian)

Division at sea and approaching the island. My intention is to land them at Soerabaya and Semarang, thus giving us three bridgeheads, one at each end and one in the middle of the island.From there we must penetrate inland to wherever the prison camps are, hopefully by negotiation but by persuasion if necessary. Dr Soekarno is understanding and helpful but he simply does not yet control the firebrands who have picked up Japanese weapons and,' he said significantly, 'have been trained to use them.'

The plan which unfolded was to land at Soerabaya on the 25th October with a Brigade and establish a firm British presence in the town. A second Brigade would then go to Semarang, a much smaller and less important town with a usable airfield. The GOC concluded by saying, short though the notice was, he would need as much air cover as we could provide for these two operations.

It did not take a mathematician to work out that the 25th was five days ahead and I did not yet have a single aircraft in Java.

We returned to the Air Commodore's office. 'Can it be done?' he asked, as he settled into his chair.

'It must be done, sir,' I replied. 'We cannot let these troops land, possibly against opposition, without air support. How far is Soerabaya?' 'About 415 miles,' said Hughie. I said that the Thunderbolts could do it with long range tanks but probably without bombs until we had tested the Kemajoran runways.

'No bombs necessary at this stage,' replied the AOC. 'One hopes that their presence will be enough but they must have a full load of ammunition in case the Army are held up.'

I learned with relief that the fuel situation could be handled as the Shell organisation still functioned in Batavia. Although the airfield fuel dump had plenty of Japanese fuel stocks, we certainly could not risk using it in the Thunderbolts. Hughie undertook to send a signal to Kuala Lumpur in Malaya to instruct my two squadrons to prepare to fly in two days time which would then give us 48 hours to prepare for the Soerabaya operation.

Java

With that settled Corporal Pattison drove the Buick back to the airfield as fast as the milling crowds of bicycles, jay walkers and mangy dogs would allow. No time now to study the delights of Batavia but, at first sight, they didn't look all that attractive. The progress made by the time I returned to the airfield was astonishing. The air was filled with the screech of tortured metal as the wrecked aircraft were dragged ruthlessly away to a far corner. Japanese labour had been mobilised and hordes of small men in khaki caps were sweeping the two runways, erecting tents which, thanks to the excellent Nichols in India, were nearly all brand new. Another band of Japanese was picking up the scraps of metal and other rubbish from the grass area between the runways where the aircraft would be parked. It was a heartening sight as I sent for Ted Cotton to go over the General's plans.

Ted was in high spirits and, after listening carefully to the plans, said: 'We can do it. Radio communication will be established by tomorrow and the control tower usable.'

He went on to tell me that he had decided to bring in the Thunderbolts on the left hand runway which had a flat and completely unobstructed approach. He thought that the other one would be preferable for our permanent use as the prevailing wind at this time of year would permit us to take off in the direction where there was a flat, marshy overshoot which should catch any aircraft with reasonable safety if it got into difficulties taking off with a load. 'But,' he said, 'we've got to do something about the surface. It will crack up rapidly under braking. We have a Japanese labour force of about 600: they are working very hard under their officers and really seem to be enjoying clearing up their own damage. I can only think that they are relieved at not receiving the harsh treatment which they have meted out to our people.'

A tour of the station revealed that order was quite rapidly appearing out of the original shambles. It was fortunate that 904 Wing possessed very experienced airmen, well accustomed to getting on with their jobs in difficult conditions under the supervision of their specialist officers. One sweating airman crawled from under a three tonner in the MT yard and we chatted as he wiped his face with cotton waste.

'A cup of char would go down well. Are we likely to get a NAAFI, sir?' he asked. 'Not for some weeks, I would think,' I replied, 'but you've given me an idea. We must try and organise some kind of "char wallah" along Indian lines to tour round every section during the morning.'

The next port of call was the street of houses which had been requisitioned for many of the troops. Basically they were quite pleasant detached villas but terribly neglected with peeling paint, unkempt gardens and, as I soon discovered, bad sewage arrangements and negligible water pressure. Nevertheless, the various units had all bedded down, five or six men to a room on camp beds. Something had to be done urgently about the water and toilet systems. I think it was the air of general neglect everywhere that had struck me particularly forcibly. The Javanese seemed to be neat and clean people and I had always imagined the Japanese to be the same, but there was no doubt that the three odd years of occupation had played havoc with community standards, certainly in Batavia. The conditions, and notably those of the canal which flowed past the station, seemed to be ideal for breeding mosquitoes, and I made a note to keep everybody on Mepacrine anti-malarial tablets as well as salt. In short, we must maintain our Ulunderpet precautions.

On the next morning, 21st October, Hughie Edwards came out to see what arrangements could be made for the Thunderbolts to fly in on the 23rd, two days before the projected operation to occupy Soerabaya. The Air Headquarters had the only communications so far set up with Singapore.

Ted and I had decided that we wanted the squadrons to arrive during the early part of the day and before the inevitable cumulus cloud started to build up. Anybody who has flown in the Far East knows how rapidly these treacherous and turbulent cloud formations can appear and build up, it is said at a speed of 1000 feet a minute up to heights of 40,000 feet. We also decided that the two squadrons should be at least one hour apart as up to 40 aircraft landing individually and with great caution on our runway would take an appreciable time. Finally, the Air Commodore wished each squadron to fly in formation over the city before landing to 'show the flag' and hopefully impress the inhabitants. All this was agreed and Hughie departed to get the necessary instructions on their way to Kuala Lumpur.

A hundred and one things remained to be done but, by the following day, the radio from the control tower was working well. We couldn't test it with an aircraft in the air as we had none, but it worked well with an Air Contact Team in a jeep outside the station. A windsock had been erected beside the tower, and the Shell Company had given us two tankers of aviation fuel while they pumped out the Japanese fuel from the storage tanks. Our doctor had checked over his ambulance and made contact with the local hospital, and the fire section was ready with firetenders and rescue equipment. My Servicing Commando would marshall the Thunderbolts after landing and look after them until the squadron airmen arrived from Kuala Lumpur by Dakota some time later. Orders had gone out that no Dakotas were to reach Kemajoran until after the Thunderbolts were safely down. That virtually meant that they were unlikely to come until the following day as we had no arrangements for night landings. All seemed to be ready and it now remained to pray for a continuation of the good weather we were having.

Our prayers were answered. The 23rd dawned with tropical splendour, blue sky with very little wind. What breeze there was would be favourable for the landings. At 7 am Hughie phoned through – the first phone connection we had had with the Air Headquarters – to say that 81 Squadron would arrive at 10 am and 60 Squadron at 11.30 am. So far so good and a final check revealed that we were as prepared to receive them as we were ever likely to be in the rough and ready conditions.

I joined Ted Cotton in the tower and we waited, and waited. At 9.45 am the controller called the squadron but there was no

72

reply, only plenty of static. He continued to call every five minutes and, at 10.10 am a faint reply was heard. An audible sigh of relief ran round the watchers. By this time, every airman who could be spared from his duties had appeared on the tarmac to watch the fun, and I fervently hoped we were not going to provide them with too many thrills.

At 10.20 am a call came from the squadron and it was so clear that Pat Kennedy's voice was quite recognisable. We had worked out the instructions to give him and these the controller read out slowly. Two green Very lights would be fired from the tower to indicate the airfield when the first aircraft was in sight. The squadron was then to fly over the city at 1000 feet, after which aircraft were to land individually on our designated runway which was 1600 yards long and rough. 'Use extreme caution and as little braking as possible' were the final instructions.

Five minutes later a low murmur was heard from the direction of the docks and the formation came into view in a shallow dive from about 3000 feet. Up went the Green lights as the formation swept past towards the city centre. 'Eighteen,' said Ted, 'three V formations of five each and one of three'. They looked fine and I heard Ted murmur, 'That ought to impress the locals'.

They disappeared in a blast of sound and again we waited, listening to Kennedy giving his instructions about landing. In a few moments the first flight of five reappeared and flew over the centre of the airfield, breaking up neatly as they passed and following their Squadron Commander round the circuit. He came in to land steadily and, for a Thunderbolt, quite slowly, touching down within twenty yards of the runway threshold. We all held our breaths to see how the runway would behave. A few stones and small pieces of tarmac could be seen flying from the wheels, but it could have been much worse as Kennedy used the whole length of the runway and obviously used very little brake. He had a highly polished uncamouflaged Thunderbolt which looked magnificent as it went past the foot of the tower with his canopy open, waving to us. At the end of the runway he was marshalled up the other one and we awaited number two. All eighteen landed without trouble, a few bumpy ones, but it was an experienced squadron and all had plenty of room to spare.

It had taken twenty five minutes to land the eighteen aircraft and it was 10.55 am by the time they were all lined up on the grass facing the flagstaff. Pat Kennedy walked over to join us in the tower, passing a few less than complimentary comments on the surface of the runways. He confirmed what most of us thought: they would not be long enough or smooth enough for full load take-offs.

Once more we waited, the controller calling 60 Squadron at five minute intervals until, at 11.20 am, a faint answering call was heard. The same procedure as before came into play, when at 11.35 am the formation was seen. It swept overhead, seventeen strong on this occasion, led by Jackie Wales, the Squadron Leader who gave us a cheery greeting as he disappeared over the city centre.

All landed safely once more but there were noticeably more loose pieces of the surface flying from their wheels. Something would have to be done – and quickly – if we were to prevent the runways from breaking up completely.

There were now thirty five Thunderbolts lined up neatly on the grass and as I looked at the space they required, I wondered how on earth we were going to accommodate twenty five Dakotas as well as visitors and probably a few more aircraft of our own. However, a start had been made and I had that satisfying feeling that once again I commanded an operational Wing, a feeling which had been absent during the voyage and our somewhat chaotic arrival in Java.

74

7

Early Operations

The day after the arrival of the Thunderbolts, 24th October, was fully occupied with seeing the Dakota squadron in and suitably parked. They came individually at about fifteen minute intervals and, like the Thunderbolts, were told to fly over the city before landing. No 31 Squadron was commanded by Wing Commander Brian Macnamara who was destined to show remarkable leadership in the humanitarian task with which his squadron was faced.

The Dakota, a military version of the Douglas DC3 civil air liner can, with no exaggeration, be described as one of the most successful aircraft of World War II. Its versatility and reliability were legendary. It was a true maid of all work, and the Burma campaign could never had been waged so successfully without the support which it gave to the troops in the jungle. It is said that, on at least one occasion in Burma, a Dakota was 'double loaded' with boxes of ammunition by accident – ammunition weighs heavily but takes up little space – but the aircraft was still able to stagger into the air before the mistake was discovered. 31 Squadron had played a full part in those tough jungle operations but came on to Java with little respite to take on its new task of rescuing the prisoners and internees.

We had decided to bring the Dakotas in on the right hand runway, and taxi them round to the one used by the Thunderbolts the previous day. That runway would then be permanently closed for flying and the large transport aircraft would be parked on the grass down one side of it. They were going to need a great deal of space for loading and unloading goods and passengers, as well as for all the essential maintenance on them which would have to be carried out in the open – not that that was any great hardship as it is doubtful whether any of them had ever had the luxury of a hangar.

They came in steadily all day at fifteen minute intervals, some twenty-two of them in all, each one loaded with a mixture of airmen and essential freight. The passengers not only included those airmen of the Thunderbolt squadrons who had remained with their aircraft during the long journey from India to Burma and Malaya and then on to Java, but also a detachment of the Royal Army Service Corps. This was an Air Dispatch Unit of soldiers whose specialised task was the loading, unloading and despatching of loads in flight during supply drops. Under their commanding officer, Lieutenant Colonel Potter, this proved to be an extremely efficient and hard working unit which thoroughly understood all the facets of operating these highly adaptable aircraft.

When I greeted Brian Macnamara and made some apology for the congestion, he said, 'This is fine. You should have seen what we have had to put up with for the last two months. My aircraft were scattered all over Malaya, Siam and Burma, and it's great to have them together again. We'll make ourselves comfortable; after all we have aircraft we can sleep in if necessary.'

While the Dakotas were flying in, a conference took place to arrange the air support for the projected occupation of Soerabaya on the following day. Hughie Edwards brought along the General's plan, which was for the 49th Infantry Brigade to land at 9 am and hopefully advance without opposition into the town. Pat Kennedy and Jackie Wales joined the discussion and we decided that a formation of six Thunderbolts would demonstrate over Soerabaya fifteen minutes before the landing, remaining overhead for half an hour, which was long as they could safely remain at that distance from home. Even to do that they would have to carry two long range tanks and cruise at their most economical speed and height. Kennedy would lead that initial formation himself. Guns would be loaded but no action was to take place unless specifically called for by the Brigade commander, Brigadier Mallaby.

Thereafter pairs of Thunderbolts would take over, showing themselves over the city for half an hour at a time throughout the hours of daylight. We made it a rule that these single seater aircraft would always fly in pairs on long or risky missions for reasons of safety and mutual support. On many later occasions we were to find this a very sound decision. Kennedy was also instructed to examine the Soerabaya airfield and gain an impression as to whether it looked suitable for Thunderbolts when the town had been occupied. As we had no alternative airfields for a diversion should a pilot get into difficulties, Wales, who would lead one of the follow-up pairs, was similarly instructed to examine the airfield at Semarang half way along the coast which was destined to be our third and last British bridgehead in the General's plan.

Several more details were agreed including the most important one of radio communication between the aircraft and 49 Brigade. Hughie expressed himself satisfied with the arrangements and departed with them to his headquarters, promising to let me know if any changes in the plan took place overnight.

When he had gone I asked the two Squadron commanders if they were happy about the endurance of the flight and about

77

taking off from our rugged runway with two overload tanks. With fingers crossed they said that they were but would Ted Cotton ensure that all the rescue and fire vehicles were in position at the far end of the runway. We finally discussed what a pilot should do if in serious difficulty with engine trouble or hit by fire from the ground. Firstly we decided that aircraft must remain at a height where they were unlikely to be hit by small arms fire. In the unusual event of engine trouble so serious that he could not get home, we agreed that the wisest thing to do was to land on the Soerabaya airfield and hope for the best. An accompanying aircraft would immediately inform 49 Brigade by radio in the hope that the Army could reach the airfield quickly.

It was clear that this operation was going to use up a great many aircraft and flying hours. My own rough calculation showed that constant cover over Soerabaya until 12.15 pm would need eighteen Thunderbolts. We had to find some means of ensuring that Brigadier Mallaby cancelled the air cover if and when he did not need it. I addressed this problem to Hughie Edwards and he told me that the General had communications with 49 Brigade and would issue instructions accordingly. As events turned out, it was fortunate that we made this provision.

Kennedy and his boys took off at 6.45 am the next morning and, although they had little to spare, they were all airborne with wheels going up before the end of the runway; disappearing into the distance. They could not be back under four hours at an economical cruising speed for conserving fuel and we had, therefore, to wait patiently for news from the 'front', despatching successive pairs at half hour intervals.

At 9.45 am, however, just as the sixth pair took off, a call came from Hughie Edwards to say that 49 Brigade had been refused permission to land but that Mallaby had informed the authorities in Soerabaya that he would land in any event at 3.15 pm. He added that the Thunderbolts were demonstrating impressively overhead but that their cover could be discontinued until 3 pm.

There was just time to recall the sixth pair who were still within radio range, and Ted Cotton stood down those preparing to follow on. Half an hour later Kennedy came on the air on his way home, giving the same information about the delayed landing and very sensibly cancelling any other aircraft which were within his radio range. They all returned, having no problem with landing on the right hand runway for the first time, being by that time quite short of fuel and lightly loaded.

Kennedy came straight to my office, looking tired and hot, but cheerful, and we got down to planning to cover the delayed landing scheduled for 3.15 pm. 'We can get there in an hour and a half at cruising speed, but I don't think we should spend more than half an hour over the target area,' said Kennedy. 'Twisting and turning at a fairly low altitude is using quite a lot of juice. We flew several times over the 'invasion fleet', anchored just off shore, and our radio reception was excellent. The town seemed to be quiet and no rifle or machine-gun fire was spotted by any of us. We then flew round the airfield which looked in better shape than this one with a few, apparently undamaged, Japanese aircraft on the tarmac. May I suggest,' he continued, 'that we send four aircraft to demonstrate reasonably aggressively from 3 pm, followed by pairs as before?'

This was agreed and we set the take-off for 1 pm to enable Jackie Wales, in this case, to be over the target comfortably by 2.45 pm. The situation at the end of the day was beginning to concern me. The only night flying equipment we possessed were some paraffin flares, reasonably adequate for experienced pilots on a full length runway but hardly sufficient under our circumstances. There was no other airfield lighting or obstruction lights and, except in an emergency, we were a daytime-only airfield.

We decided that 6.30 pm must be the final landing time for the last pair, which meant leaving Soerabaya at 5 o'clock and I asked that the final pair be thoroughly experienced pilots in case darkness overtook them on return.

As our conference ended a further signal came through from 49 Brigade stating that the Indonesians had accepted the Brigadier's ultimatum and that the landing would go ahead at 3.15 pm. We despatched our next wave of aircraft as planned, Wales being instructed to look at the Semarang airfield on his way home. The afternoon was quiet with the last pairs going off to time and we awaited their return with interest, getting the paraffin flares positioned down the runway as a precaution against a late arrival or a lame duck.

Jackie Wales and his flight roared overhead at 4.40 pm and treated us to a spectacular break up and landing. He reported that the Brigade was landing in Soerabaya harbour as he left and there appeared to be no discernible opposition in the town, but he reckoned that he could see Indonesians with arms retreating inland from the outskirts. This turned out later to be a true report.

Semarang, he thought, was too small for Thunderbolts except in emergency but looked as if it would be satisfactory for Dakotas. It was obviously not a well-developed airfield and there were no signs of Japanese aircraft on it. It seemed to be deserted. Our last aircraft landed as the sun was setting, which concluded a satisfactory day: even more satisfactory when Air Headquarters rang me up to say that the Brigade had landed without opposition and was consolidating in the dock area. Brigadier Mallaby was good enough to add that he considered the lack of opposition was largely due to the timely arrival of the Thunderbolts. The two squadrons were jubilant and celebrated suitably that evening, as indeed we did in the Wing Mess where the level of the *Llanstephan Castle* case of gin dropped significantly.

This first day of operations had used the resources of twenty four Thunderbolts and, successful though they had been, it was quite clear that we could not operate at that intensity and at that range indefinitely. Something had to be done to keep the effort at a practicable level. My mind turned to the idea that, if 49 Brigade occupied the Soerabaya airfield and it turned out to be suitable for the operation of Thunderbolts, we ought to send some down there on detachment to cover the further operations of the Brigade which would undoubtedly try to deploy out to the areas thought to house some of the prisoner-of-war camps.

While we were discussing this possibility over our gin that evening, a call came through from Edwards to the effect that we were to be reinforced with some Mosquitos from Singapore, two detachments of the bomber version and one of rocket firing aircraft. They would probably arrive the next day. It then transpired that Brigadier Mallaby's troops had been held up after landing and were having to fight their way into the centre of Soerabaya. Apparently there were hordes of fanatical Indonesians, well armed with automatic weapons, Bofors anti-aircraft guns and even a few armoured personnel carriers. This was indeed bad news, but worse was to come. During the next day Mallaby himself was brutally murdered while attempting to negotiate with the Indonesian authorities. There was now no doubt that Dr Soekarno and his government had no control over the more distant parts of the island.

This was not the only bad news. Air Commodore Stevens sent an Australian Wing Commander from his staff and several airmen down there at once and they were captured by Indonesians while attempting to reach the airfield and flung into a jail where the conditions were unspeakable. As expected, they had been mistaken for Dutch and it took two days for the Australian to persuade his captors who they were and obtain their release.

The Brigade then called for an air strike on various targets where the Indonesians had taken up defensive positions on the outskirts of the town. The task had to be accepted and my two squadron commanders decided that they could reduce their fuel loads and carry a bomb load provided that they could fly direct to their targets, waste no time and return immediately.

In the cool of the morning, twelve Thunderbolts took off safely, with sighs of relief from all the onlookers, which meant most of the Wing. Three and a quarter hours later Wales, who was leading them, came on the air, saying that all was well, the mission had been successful and he was breaking the formation up early so that they could land without delay. Ten minutes later they came round the airfield in a long stream and landed one by one. Shortly afterwards we heard that the targets had either been demolished or severely damaged and the Indonesian forces were retiring out into the country. The Brigade hoped to occupy the airfield within hours.

At around noon the Mosquitos began to arrive from Singapore. They came from three different squadrons – eight of the bomber version and four equipped with rocket projectiles. They were commanded and led by Wing Commander Michael Constable-Maxwell, a seasoned campaigner with a DSO and a DFC who was, in fact, the commanding officer of 84 Squadron and had four aircraft of his squadron with him. They had no problems with our runway and we managed to squeeze them in at one end of the out-of-use runway beyond the line of parked Dakotas. The airfield was now getting uncomfortably full with between eighty and a hundred aircraft, but I was delighted to see this addition to the Wing which would add much more versatility to our operational possibilities. Maxwell was also delighted about joining the Wing as he said that Singapore was desperately crowded and not a happy place, with very little useful flying to be done. He was highly experienced as his decorations proved, an extremely able and intelligent officer who soon proved himself to be one of the mainstays of the station. Within hours of arrival he had organised his squadron into tents provided for him close to the Mosquitos, sorted out accommodation for his troops close to the station and found an Officers' Mess in the town.

'Now,' he said next morning, 'we want some work to do.'

That was not at all difficult and some of his aircraft were despatched to Soerabaya to demonstrate over the town and make contact with 49 Brigade which was still being held up and awaiting reinforcements which were on the way.

The closing days of October were intensely active as attention switched back to the Batavia bridgehead. The area held by British forces was intended to encompass the two towns of Bandoeng and Buitenzorg. The former had been the commercial capital of Java, situated up in the hills some fifty miles away. It contained a large number of prisoners and internees who were being held by fanatical Indonesians and starved of food and other supplies. Two large formations of Thunderbolts were sent to demonstrate over the town with Dakotas dropping leaflets calling for a surrender. The single runway airfield appeared, in this instance, to be in good condition with a long line of apparently undamaged Japanese Zero fighters lined up along one side of it.

The problem now was how to occupy Bandoeng and get supplies rapidly to the population as well as to rescue the prisoners. A railway ran between Batavia and Bandoeng and General Christison decided to send a heavily escorted train through, loaded with food and medical supplies. In spite of the armed escort from 23 Division, it was ambushed en route and many of the Ghurka guards were killed, only one wagon reaching its destination. The railway was clearly much too dangerous to use, running as it did through isolated hilly country which was ideal for ambushes. Supply by air and road convoys with full air cover was decided upon. Bandoeng itself, which contained representatives of Dr Soekarno's government and a detachment of RAPWI was relatively quiet, guerrilla activity being largely confined to the neighbouring countryside.

A regular flow of Dakotas carrying supplies in and prisoners out was established with sufficient British and Ghurka troops to secure the airfield and protect the unloading and reloading of the aircraft. Road convoys with powerful air cover by Mosquitos and Thunderbolts were also started but it was not long before a convoy became engaged in a pitched battle despite the efforts of escorting fighters to drive off the Indonesians by machine gun and rocket attack directed by a 904 Wing Air Contact Team in their jeep. Both RAF occupants of the jeep were killed as well as many troops of the convoy escort.

After these two disasters the responsibility for supplying Bandoeng devolved upon the Dakotas which started regular delivery flights, taking 425 tons of food and supplies up to the beleaguered town each week and bringing back hundreds of prisoners and internees. Even then tragedy struck as the fanatics turned upon the prison camps and perpetrated many atrocities before the inmates could be rescued, including one appalling incident in which fourteen internees, some of them women, were locked in a house and burned to death. A strike by Mosquitos and Thunderbolts on a number of targets in Bandoeng, identified as being used by the guerrilla forces, created a great deal of damage and caused some subsequent reduction in the hostile activity. But the situation was extremely serious, the worst feature being that the very people we were trying to rescue became the targets for fanatical violence.

General Christison had at his disposal only two Divisions of troops and he assessed that about eight would be needed to quell the whole island. In view of the demands of all the other areas of South East Asia to be occupied, no more troops could be made available for Java. Fortunately the third bridgehead at Semarang on the coast half way between Batavia and Soerabaya was occupied by one of the General's brigades without any opposition and, as it contained a useful airfield, it gave us another evacuation point with a small port to which prisoners could be flown. It also provided a valuable and well positioned airfield for aircraft in difficulties.

So within a few weeks of our arrival, the three bridgeheads had been established but not without difficulty and numerous casualties. My wing had already had three killed, two on the Bandoeng road; and one airman shot in Batavia itself, which had alerted us to the dangers of urban guerrillas.

By mid-November, after two more brigades had strengthened the force in Soerabaya, I was ready to send a detachment of aircraft to the airfield there. Eight Thunderbolts of 60

Squadron and two bomber Mosquitos, all under the command of Wing Commander Maxwell and supplied by our Dakotas, flew down and immediately started operating in support of the Army, now under the command of General Mansergh. This was an immense relief and removed from my shoulders responsibility for providing at least operational air support for that distant bridgehead. But we had been lucky, as a number of Thunderbolts and also Dakotas had been hit by rifle and machine gun fire. None had been so severely damaged that they were unable to return to Kemajoran, but the possibility of an even more serious incident was ever present.

Looking back over these early operations, it was quite clear that 904 Wing was involved in yet another war and had walked into a situation which had been totally unexpected when we sailed peacefully from Madras only a few weeks earlier. Although we were beginning to get many prisoners and internees out from the readily accessible camps, there were many more thousands in camps in the interior with which no contact had yet been made. We could not hope to reach them by force. Even if the troops were available, which was not the case, the chances were that the inmates would be massacred before they could be reached. Long and difficult negotiations were the only solution and, of course, they were already under way.

I was now convinced that my Wing was in for quite a long stay in Java and had to take steps to improve conditions at Kemajoran, which we had made operable, but which was far from comfortable.

8

The Runway

These early operations showed without doubt that our single runway would not stand up to intensive use by heavy aircraft indefinitely. Every landing and take-off was accompanied by a scattering of loose pieces of the top surface and sweeping was a daily routine by gangs of our Japanese labour force. Punctures were fortunately few and far between but the danger of a high speed burst on a Thunderbolt was an ever present danger which could easily result in a serious accident. The Mosquito with its wood and ply construction with a low and vulnerable tailplane was the most likely to receive damage from stones thrown up by the wheels. The Dakota, on the other hand, was perhaps the least likely to be damaged by debris or a tyre burst.

Air Headquarters was as concerned as I was about this state of affairs, and had already made urgent requests to Singapore for a senior Works Engineer to be sent to Java to advise on measures to be taken. I am bound to say that the response was heartening and a Mr Atkinson was appointed to undertake the task, arriving by our daily Dakota from Singapore with commendable speed on 8th November. I met him as he disembarked and drove him slowly to our Mess for a wash and brush-up, having managed to make a room available for him.

'My goodness,' he said as we drove round the tarmac while he surveyed the mass of aircraft occupying almost every available parking space, 'I don't think Singapore realises what is going on here. I thought the airfields there were congested, but not to this extent.'

I had instructed Ted Cotton to stop all flying for half an hour, except for emergencies, while Atkinson and I inspected the runway. We walked slowly down it, pausing at intervals while he bent down and picked up pieces of the loose surface. 'Hmm,' he muttered, 'very poor quality stuff. I'm not surprised it's breaking up.' Turning to me: 'How long do you expect to be here?' 'I really have little idea,' I replied, 'but in view of the situation, I cannot see our getting out under six to eight months, and it seems to me that things could well drag on for a year.' 'Well,' he said picking up another handful of runway, 'this certainly won't last that time if, as you said earlier, your movements up and down the runway amount to sixty to eighty a day.' We walked slowly back to my office, pausing to watch a Mosquito land with the usual scattering of small pieces of tarmac from its wheels. Atkinson shook his head. 'There's no doubt you have a problem, Group Captain, which I fear I am about to inherit.' I hoped so too, but I didn't say anything.

He settled into a thoroughly uncomfortable chair which was all my office could offer and he put his finger tips together, for all the world like a Bishop about to commence a sermon, looked at me and said, 'Firstly, I take it there is no question of putting the runway out of action while we work on it?' I shook my head. He went on, 'Complete resurfacing with tarmac is also out of the question. It would take at least a thousand tons and even if that quantity were available, which I very much doubt, it would be impracticable to do without putting the runway out of action. Patching would be useless and might even accelerate the break up of the unpatched parts.' He paused, thinking deeply while shifting in his uncomfortable chair. 'What about PSP*?' I asked.

He shook his head vigorously. 'There isn't enough in the theatre, nor is there shipping to spare to bring the large quantity needed to Java. There are other problems with PSP. We have just covered the main runway at Changri (Singapore) with it, Changri having been built on a marsh by the Japanese, using Allied prisoners as labour. They managed to sabotage the construction in small ways, drainage and so forth, and so we have used what PSP was available to rectify the damage. Even so, flying has to cease for two days a week while the PSP is tightened and straightened. You would hardly believe it, but when a heavy aircraft lands, it pushes a wave of PSP, several inches high, in front of it as it slows down. Five days of that and the metal is loose and out of shape.'

I was obviously beginning to look dejected, but Atkinson said: 'Don't worry, I've been in airfield construction all my life and I won't be beaten by this problem.' He thought deeply again, tapping his pointed fingers together.

'Bit Hess is the answer,' he suddenly said cheerfully. I was puzzled. 'Bit Hess?' I queried.

'Bitumised Hessian – sheets of jute, hessian or sacking which is soaked in tar and then laid in sheets, several thicknesses deep over the whole runway surface. This binds the under-surface together, is completely waterproof and makes a durable and pliable landing surface – like landing on a mattress', he said as an afterthought. 'That's the answer.'

'It sounds odd to me,' I said, 'but you are the expert. How do you get supplies of material?'

---

*PSP – Pierced Steel Planking is made of interlocking metal mesh which can be laid on top of a reasonably firm surface and helps to preserve the material underneath.

Atkinson went on to assure me that supply would be no problem. The hessian came from India and he had stocks of it in Singapore. Treating it with bitumen would be done on the spot here and laying it was a relatively unskilled job providing that it was supervised. By this time his cheerful confidence was beginning to affect me and a solution to our difficult problem seemed to be in sight. However, that was not the end of our discussion.

'How are you going to lay the Bit Hess?' I asked, 'because the runway must be kept in use by day. Can you do the work in sections by night?'

He replied that that would not be acceptable as the new surface would take a day or two to dry or the aircraft would pick up wet tar and produce an appalling mess.

'You have a pretty wide runway,' he said, 'and if we divide it down the centre line, working on one side at a time, can you land on the other half? We would, of course, mark the dividing line with cones or low barrels so that a wing overlapping them would not be damaged. There is one final problem – that of maintaining the Bit Hess. Pieces of it will, from time to time, be picked up by the aircraft and perhaps torn away from the surface. I suggest that one or two of your Japanese be stationed alongside the runway with buckets of tar and brushes, ready to rush out and stick down any piece which has been pulled up.'

It seemed to me that this solution of the problem contained all the characteristics of Heath Robinson, but at least it was an answer, and Atkinson clearly knew his business. We had a break while I sent for my four squadron commanders, and then outlined the proposal to them and, in particular, the risks involved in using half the width of the runway. To my surprise they were not as taken aback as I had been: two of them knew about Bit Hess, and had seen some of it in use in the Burmese jungle. Macnamara had even landed a Dakota on it, laid over a hard dust surface. He had liked it and was quite enthusiastic about Atkinson's scheme. All four agreed that the restricted take off and landing arrangements would be acceptable with great care for a short period. 'No problem for the Thunderbolts', said both Kennedy and Wales. Macnamara said that the only difficulty with Dakotas was the size of their wing span which might occasionally cause a wing tip to overlap the centre line.

'We ought to have a man with a whistle, like the railways, to warn the workers of an approaching aircraft, so that they could draw back for a moment,' suggested Macnamara.

Mosquitos also appeared to present no real problems and any tendency they had to swing slightly on take off was easily corrected. Visiting aircraft which came mostly from Singapore would have to be warned by the issue of a Notice to Airmen and briefed by radio when overhead.

Mr Atkinson then interjected, 'There will be five or six layers of this material on the surface. It will be extremely pliable which means that it will form small ridges and hollows as it settles down. After heavy rain, it will probably puddle as there is little or no camber on this runway to take the water away to the sides. There will be no serious effect but you must expect sheets of spray to be thrown up on landing.'

That seemed to be all there was to discuss and Atkinson said he would like to get back to Singapore to start the project. He undertook to send an experienced engineer from his staff to supervise and possibly a few airmen from the RAF Airfield Construction Branch. As far as labour was concerned, he hoped that we would use the Japanese as he was doing on the Singapore airfields. Controlled by their own officers, they were working very well. The first instalment of Bit Hess would come by Dakota, but he hoped to find shipping available to bring in the main load.

As I drove him out to his aircraft the following day a Dakota load of internees landed from Bandoeng and I said he might like to see what came out of the aircraft to get some idea of the work we were doing. I couldn't have chosen a more suitable moment as twenty five poor souls emerged. Half a dozen were on stretchers and almost all had to be helped carefully down the steps. Haggard and emaciated as they all were, with swollen limbs indicating beri-beri, they were nevertheless thrilled and delighted to be free after several years of terrible confinement. Atkinson was deeply impressed, as I knew he would be, and he boarded his aircraft, assuring me that he would not lose a moment in helping us with our task.

He was as good as his word. Within five days a young and energetic engineer with six Airfield Construction Squadron airmen duly arrived in a Dakota, fully loaded with Bit Hess and barrels of tar, so that an immediate start could be made. The rains, which I knew were likely to come before Christmas, had held off so far, but there was great urgency to get on with the job while the excellent weather continued.

Work immediately started on marking out the centre line of the runway, using drums cut in half, filled with water and painted white. One or two problems immediately arose. Covering the turning circles at each end of the runway would have to be left for the final stages as half a turning circle was insufficient for the Dakotas. Also a way had to be found to taxi aircraft on and off the section to be used, but these and other minor snags were ironed out without too much difficulty.

The next important step was to test that the half runway was adequate for the different types of aircraft. Accordingly test flights were conducted with our three aircraft types before work actually began. Kennedy and Wales both confirmed that the Thunderbolt was happy enough. Macnamara said, 'It's a bit tight but acceptable and it will make the boys fly accurately and keep straight. However, I do think our warning whistle is essential as a wing tip may easily overlap the barrels by a foot or two.' The Mosquito pilot said exactly the same but was quite happy to accept the situation.

We could not reduce flying by very much as it was nearly all urgent and essentially operational. Nevertheless we did ban any flights which were not necessary, and that included me. I had not so far flown at Kemajoran owing to the pressure of work and I was dying to take the Wing Thunderbolt up and look around the countryside.

91

The work started immediately the half runway in use had been declared fit and the necessary safety instructions sent out. A strong smell of tar now pervaded the station and it was fascinating to watch the Japanese carpeting the surface with layer upon layer of Bit Hess under the watchful eye of the six Airfield Construction airmen who told me that they had little experience of using the material. 'And nasty stuff it is to handle too,' said one of them as I discussed it with them. In the remarkably short time of a week, the first half was finished but had to be left for two days to dry and consolidate. When newly laid it presented a shiny jet black surface but the shine soon disappeared in use.

The two halves were then changed over and, with new supplies coming in, the second half was also completed in a week plus a couple of days to dry. In order to cover the two turning circles, which had broken up badly due to the twisting action of the tyres, it was necessary to bring the full runway into use, instructing pilots to turn round on the runway itself while the circles were being treated one at a time. There was some additional risk here as aircraft had to come in very low indeed over the circle being worked on and the warning whistle assumed even greater importance.

It all worked well so that, within three weeks, a brand new runway was available and in use. Although I had not yet tried it out myself, all the pilots were delighted with the soft and comfortable landing it gave them. The question was, however, would it stand up to sixty to eighty movements a day for the duration of our stay? Mr Atkinson came along to examine the completed work and said he was pleased with the result.

'I am sure it will stand up to your traffic for a year or so provided that it gets the constant maintenance it will undoubtedly need. You see that?' he asked, pointing to a strip of Bit Hess which was standing a little proud of the rest. 'That will probably come up after a landing and must be stuck down again at once.' Our Japanese, with tar buckets and brushes were already in position down both sides of the strip and this was a system which we had to continue for the next ten months or so. How fortunate it was that we had the Japanese to use for the purpose.

The time had come for me to try out the runway for myself and so, early one morning, I taxied the Wing Thunderbolt out onto the turning circle and could already feel what a cushioning effect the new surface had. Not having flown for almost three months, I carried out the pre-take off checks and roared off down the runway, not forgetting on this occasion to operate the water-injection at the right moment. Lightly loaded and without long range tanks, she shot into the air in about a thousand yards.

First of all I had a good look at the city from 3000 feet. It was even larger than I had thought, and the densely packed Chinese quarter was very evident, teeming with scurrying figures and bicycles by the thousand. I then had a look at the docks where we had landed. The devastation was plain to see. Nevertheless a lot of shipping was coming to life again after the sterile years of occupation. Flying inland for a while the countryside was lush with market gardens and fruit trees in profusion. What looked like coffee, rice and tobacco from my height seemed to predominate as I flew almost up to Bandoeng before turning back towards the sea.

Long sandy beaches, fringed with coconut palms, extended as far as I could see towards Semarang, but I was particularly interested in some islands a few miles offshore. There are alleged to be a thousand islands stretching in a long chain towards Singapore. One of them attracted my interest and I dropped to 1000 feet to look at it closely. It had no name on my map but subsequently it turned out to be called Eden island. No name could have been more appropriate. About one mile square and four miles offshore, it was surrounded by clean, beautiful beaches with water so clear that I could easily see the bottom. The island was covered with the ubiquitous coconuts and also bananas. However, what interested me was the tall relic of what looked like an old lighthouse and several derelict huts or brick buildings around. There was no sign of life and it was obviously uninhabited. What a place for a picnic or a brief holiday, I thought to myself as the Thunderbolt quietly drifted round it at 150 knots.

An idea was taking shape in my mind. I was concerned that we had no means of giving the airmen leave away from the station and a time would come when arrangements ought to be made to let at least some of them get away for short periods. I made a mental note to look into the Eden island situation as I could see, even from the air, that it would be an ideal place for small parties of airmen to camp, swim, fish and generally look after themselves for a few days. So excited was I by this prospect that I forgot where I was going until I pulled myself together and realised that I was flying in the opposite direction to Batavia.

Now for a perfect landing on the new runway. I flew back to the circuit, called the tower and received landing instructions. The controller knew the 'old man' was flying and gave me immediate clearance, wind speed and direction, etc. The runway looked very clean and smart as I turned into the wind, made a reasonable approach and landed on the feather mattress. It really was soft and yielding and, furthermore, seemed to me to have some braking effect as I found it necessary to use very little brake before coming to rest.

As I climbed out of my aircraft, I was surprised to see Air Commodore Stevens walking towards me. I hadn't expected him, and apologised for not being there to meet him.

'Not at all; I thought I would come out on the spur of the moment to look at this new runway. You seemed happy enough with it as you came in to land.'

'At the moment I think it is splendid but it remains to be seen how it will stand up to our wear and tear. We are going to be highly dependent on our Japanese to carry out repairs – if necessary after every landing.'

'Well,' said the AOC, 'if we have to send the Japanese home before we leave – and there is not much hope of that owing to the desperate shortage of shipping – I am sure we can get some local Javanese labour to replace them.'

Even as we chatted, a Dakota landed and a long strip of Bit Hess flew up behind it, almost, but not quite wrapping itself round the tailplane. We watched as a small Japanese figure rushed out with his brush and bucket to stick it back in place again. Well, we had been warned that this would occur, as indeed it did on many occasions, but our remedial measures worked well. As the Bit Hess consolidated under the weight of aircraft, these occasions tended to decrease and it was a comfort to know that they were unlikely to cause accidents. And Mr Atkinson had been quite right about landings in wet weather. Dakotas, in particular, landed like destroyers – sheets of spray shooting from the wheels as they touched down. They needed little or no braking to pull them up.

Before he departed I told the Air Commodore that I thought it was a great tribute to the ingenuity of Mr Atkinson and his engineers who had devised this solution to what was probably our biggest problem. He agreed and promised to write to Singapore accordingly.

9

Settling in at Kemajoran

While the runway was undergoing its facelift, a great effort was being made to make the station more comfortable and more efficient, always mindful of the fact that heavy rains could be confidently expected by Christmas.

One of the most unusual problems concerned money. Not that any of the officers or airmen were short of cash, but we soon discovered that the currency we had was unacceptable. Batavian shopkeepers would not, understandably, accept Dutch money nor, in view of the suspicion which existed about the British presence, would they take sterling.

The airmen were allowed into the city, although later on we had to impose a night time curfew for all British personnel, but they found themselves unable to buy the simple necessities such as soap, toothpaste and razor blades, let alone be able to have a Chinese meal, which was a particular attraction.

My Accountant Officer came to see me in a very perturbed state. 'I don't know how to pay the troops,' he said.'I have five different currencies in my safes and only one of them is acceptable to the locals.'

'Which one is that?' I asked.

'The Japanese guilder.'

'I beg your pardon,' I said, unable to believe my ears.

He explained that the Japanese had produced their own currency based on the Dutch guilder and it had been forced upon the Javanese tradesmen as the only legal tender during the occupation. He told me that he and the Air Headquarters' accounts staff had sacks full of these notes which had been taken over on our arrival. This was a poser as it was clear that we could not expect the NAAFI to set up shop here until it was firmly established in Singapore. In any case the men were fully entitled to spend their pay on goods and entertainment other than what NAAFI could provide. I asked whether he or the AOC's staff had any proposals to make.

'Well, sir,' he said, 'it sounds very odd but we can only suggest that small quantities of this Japanese money is issued weekly to everybody until such time as an acceptable currency is negotiated.'

'Just hand it out, free of charge?' I enquired.

'Yes.'

'Well, who is going to redeem it?'

'A good question which nobody can answer at the moment,' he said. 'This money is, of course, worthless but if it's all the Indonesians will accept, it will presumably be up to them to obtain redemption in due course.'

I admitted to being staggered by this proposal, but the more I thought it over the more convinced I became that it was the only feasible solution. My Accountant interrupted my thoughts.

'Of course, we will continue to pay the men their normal wages in sterling and this extra 'gift' will be small, say ten pounds a week, purely for use in making purchases in the town. All our internal charges, mess bills, etc, will continue to be paid in sterling as they always have been. I believe,' he continued, 'that both General Christison and the Air Commodore are aware of this idea, and are thought, obviously with some reluctance, to agree with it.'

I could understand the airmen, and indeed the officers, getting pretty hot under the collar if the present situation persisted and so I decided to get along to Air Headquarters and discuss it urgently. A long and very difficult meeting took place in the General's office – difficult not because of any dis-agreement but because the idea of issuing what was virtually worthless money could have far reaching repercussions at higher levels. Eventually General Christison, who had far more troops under his command than we had and had already seen the size of the problem, decided that he must authorise the issue of modest sums to everybody for the briefest possible period. His mind was made up when one of his senior staff officers said that he had been in contact with the NAAFI authorities in Singapore, and there was no hope of a NAAFI organisation setting up shop in Java before Christmas. Their supplies would probably have to come direct from India and, although the goods were available there, the shipping was not. The General approved the scheme and concluded the meeting by telling us that he would tackle the Indonesian government about the lack of co-operation on currency matters and the risk that troops might, if pushed too far, take matters into their own hands and begin to threaten shopkeepers. It was finally agreed that the issue of Japanese currency would be modest and limited to the equivalent of £10 per week for officers and troops alike.

As soon as I returned to Kemajoran, I addressed the airmen in the dining hall at lunchtime. The decision was met with a roar of laughter and loud cheers. I emphasised that it was intended to buy essentials only but that it might stretch to a Chinese meal once a week to supplement the delicious messing they were getting – another loud cheer. I too, indulged in a Chinese meal with my colleagues from time to time, and delicious they were in the Chinese quarter of the city. Frogs' legs were a speciality which I had never experienced and two or three officers and I would take the Buick into Chinatown to get some relief from the inevitable compo rations which were still our staple diet.

While discussing the money question with the AOC, he raised a completely different subject, namely the problem posed by the thousands of women interned in camps in Batavia itself. They had all been separated from husbands who were still locked up in various camps throughout the island, some of which had not been identified, let alone reached. An immediate step had been taken to remove the Japanese guards from the women's camps, replace them mainly with Ghurkas and pour in as much food as possible.

There was thought to be more than 50,000 of these unfortunate women and it would take some considerable time to get them away from the island, reunited with their husbands where possible and restored to normal life. With the situation as it was, they could not possibly be given the free run of the city and the British forces were as much responsible for their safety as for that of the menfolk.

The Air Commodore said that it had been decided to allocate each of these camps to a regiment or unit, not to guard them but to provide any help or comfort to them in their distressing situation.

'I would like 904 Wing to take on Adek camp on the outskirts of the city,' he said. 'You and some of your officers and men could visit Adek and possibly get a few suitably qualified women to come out daily to work for you. Many of them are well educated and could doubtless help with accountancy, secretarial work, etc, but they must be returned to Adek each night and, of course, fetched by transport in the mornings.' I told him that we would do our best but doubted whether we could suitably employ more than half a dozen.

George Rumsey and I decided to visit the camp on the following day, finding it eventually with some difficulty on the opposite side of the city. A smart Ghurka soldier was on duty at the gates and, having identified ourselves, he unlocked the heavily padlocked gates. I was fully expecting to find a scene of some squalor and degradation, but was pleasantly surprised. The camp, consisting of rows of huts, was scrupulously clean and tidy. A middle aged Dutch woman who, like most Dutch people, spoke excellent English, came out to meet us and introduced herself as the unofficial camp leader. She took us into several of the huts which were grossly overcrowded but nevertheless neat and clean. I counted sixty five crowded into one hut, all delighted to see us but looking thin and ill with all the signs of semi starvation. But their spirit was indomitable, now buoyed up by the prospect of freedom.

They comprised a mixture of nationalities: some pure Dutch or 'Hollanders' as they were known, many East Indies Dutch, the result of inter-marriage, a few Swiss and even some Australians. At least two thirds of them had husbands interned elsewhere and I could only assure them that we would rescue their menfolk as fast as we could reach them and bring them out. A few, but a very few families had already been re-united and they would be the first to be repatriated. One woman, who was probably only about thirty but looked almost twice that age, told me that she had been made to walk a hundred miles in bare feet to reach Adek but, she said, 'I managed to bring two dresses and some make-up.' I shook my head. What could you say to such courage and cheerfulness?

George and I then retired to the leader's hut to discuss with her what we could possibly do to help.

'Well,' she said, 'Firstly send small parties of your men along to talk to them and tell them what's going on in the outside world, bring any spare books you may have, writing paper and materials: but chatting to them will be quite the best therapy after these terrible years. I don't think we will be here too much longer as I understand from the Army that some of the hotels in the town are being opened up to house internees until they can be repatriated.'

100

'Now,' I said, 'we could employ a few out at Kemajoran on a daily basis.' At this point George produced a short list of the duties we had thought suitable and in which extra help would be a valuable bonus.

'In addition,' George said, 'I am pretty sure that Joan Vickers, our Red Cross chief,* would welcome some help with the internees as they arrive on the airfield. We would, of course, collect them with our transport and with a guard at, say, six o'clock each morning, feed them well and return them in the evening or earlier.'

We left our list with the leader, whose name I never did discover, and she promised to select people with suitable qualifications for the jobs we had in mind. She was most grateful and that established a bond with Adek which we maintained for the few further months of the camp's existence.

As we drove back to Kemajoran we discussed how to arrange for small groups of our men to visit the camp.

'I think they must be volunteers with a good sprinkling of NCOs among them,' said George. I left it to him to organise and the result was very satisfactory – about half a dozen officers and airmen went to Adek on most days when they could be spared and, although somewhat overawed at first by the sheer numbers of women, they soon lost their shyness and regaled the ladies with tales of the war and their own experiences. They were good ambassadors.

When our helpers arrived for the first time two days after my visit, we allocated them, one to the doctor, another to the chaplain who was trying to convert a derelict building into a church, another to the Intelligence section, and so on.

For me the greatest success was to find a young Dutch girl who was prepared to be our 'tea lady' or 'char wallah' as the airmen preferred to call her. She could drive – just, and we

---

*Joan Vickers was head of the Red Cross organisation and later became Dame Joan Vickers and Member of Parliament for Plymouth (Devonport). She was then created Baroness.

entrusted her with one of the Japanese light trucks equipped with a large tea urn and buns if the cooks could produce them. Her name was Miep and she toured round the camp during duty hours distributing 'char and wads' with strict instructions never to drive close to an aeroplane or go out on the runway. This was perhaps the most popular innovation we ever introduced and I couldn't help but notice that the airman who gave her the initial driving instructions and showed her the way round was the same fitter with whom I had discussed the need for a 'char wallah' some weeks earlier in the transport yard.

One morning Sorel-Cameron arrived with a brand new RAF flag under his arm. 'With the AOC's compliments', handing it over to me. 'He greatly admires your initiative but cannot stand the sight of your home-made one. He would be grateful if you would replace it at once, if not sooner.' 'OK Sorel,' I replied. 'Will you on behalf of the AOC do me the honour of hoisting it?' I sent for the Orderly Sergeant who lowered our old flag and hoisted the new one while Sorel and I stood at the salute. I kept our old flag to begin with for sentimental reasons, but eventually had it draped over a Memorial tablet which was created in our workshops in memory of all those who died in 904 Wing while in Java.

It was fortunate that the RAF flag had to be lowered at sunset as we entered a phase when the local natives tried to steal every piece of cloth they could lay their hands on. Clothing was one of the scarcest commodities: every piece of cloth, however harsh in texture, being extremely valuable.

Twice in one week daring young natives managed to climb up and remove the windsock from its pole despite the routine patrols of the Regiment guards. The last straw was an incident one night involving the guards on the petrol dump and bomb dumps over on the far side of the airfield. The Corporal in charge of the guard was sitting in his tent writing a letter to his girl friend by the light of a hurricane lamp, with his loaded rifle lying beside him. Suddenly he heard a scratching noise outside. He took little notice thinking it was some small animal prowling round. The noise continued, however, and so he got up to look outside, unfortunately leaving his rifle behind. To his horror an Indonesian had just finished cutting all the outer panels of canvas from his tent, leaving him sitting in the inner skin. By the time he had retrieved his rifle, which he should never have left behind, the villain had bolted and none of the guards saw him or were able to trace him. Needless to say there were some pretty red necks in the RAF Regiment the next morning. The Squadron Commander was furious but, in fact, the incident had its value and showed very clearly the cunning and thieving we were up against on a large airfield with totally inadequate boundary protection. We solved the problem of the windsock by wrapping barbed wire round the pole, but that made it increasingly difficult to replace the canvas sleeve when necessary. It certainly stopped the thefts.

The next incident of this kind was an arson attempt to set fire to the petrol storage area. Late one afternoon the long grass between the fuel dump and the boundary was seen to be blazing. The fire section was very quickly on the scene as the fire tender stationed by the control tower was no more than a few hundred yards away. The fire was extinguished long before there was any danger to the fuel storage, but two cans of paraffin were found nearby and it was undoubtedly a deliberate attempt to set fire to the fuel. It was a pretty amateurish attempt as the wind was blowing away from the fuel and it was carried out at a time when it was certain to be spotted from the tower at once.

We were convinced that these incidents were the work of local natives until some nights later a young Regiment airman was shot and killed at his post on the perimeter from a shot outside the boundary fence. His colleagues of the guard scoured the immediate area but found nothing. This was unlikely to have been the work of the local inhabitants, and so it looked as if the Indonesian fanatics had decided to include the airfield on their list of targets. Guards were strengthened in every possible way including constant patrolling by two armoured cars which the Regiment possessed.

103

The funeral of the young Regiment airman was held on the day after his death and a special plot had been reserved for military graves in the city cemetery. But for the courage and leadership of a Regiment NCO, Sergeant Williams, who was commanding the firing party, this would have ended in further tragedy. I, with other members of the Wing, was following the cortege into the cemetery when fire was opened up upon us from behind a hedge one hundred yards away. We all fell flat on our faces while Sergeant Williams shouted to the coffin bearers to drop it and hide behind it. Telling us all to remain flat, he took his firing party crawling towards the point from which the fire had come, using the gravestones as cover. He ordered his men to load with live ammunition and fired several shots into the hedge, but two natives were eventually seen running away in the distance, well out of range. Leaving a couple of airmen on guard by the hedge, our chaplain, supported by a now rather dirty and dishevelled party of mourners, completed the burial as quickly as possible and left hastily.

That was the last funeral we had in the city cemetery. Our chaplain consecrated a plot inside the airfield by the main entrance and I am sorry to say that we had to bury quite a number of members of 904 Wing there temporarily during the next few months. Sergeant Williams was subsequently awarded the Military Medal which he richly deserved for his very rapid reaction and conduct throughout the incident.

Security was becoming a real worry and, although the Indonesian government was alleged to have control of Batavia, the frequent anti-British incidents proved this not to be so. Guard duties, particularly at night, were over-stretching my two Regiment squadrons and I was compelled to ask the operational squadrons to provide airmen to guard their own aircraft at night, and also put a few men from other units of the station on some static duties, such as guarding the main gates. The disaffection and number of incidents in the city had reached a level at which General Christison decided to impose a dusk to dawn curfew – a severe restriction but a very wise move for which I was grateful as RAF personnel were likely to be shot at any time when shopping or having a drink with their Japanese money. A handful of senior officers, of which I was one, were issued with special passes allowing us out during curfew hours if the need arose for urgent military conferences, etc. Fortunately the curfew did not last indefinitely as, after Christmas, the internal security situation improved and it could be lifted.

The curfew was extremely awkward for the majority of the airmen who were living in the street of houses which had been commandeered initially. It was admittedly no more than half a mile from the camp but it was not always possible for the men to get back to their houses before dark and special transport arrangements had to be made. These houses were a headache for two reasons. Firstly, the toilet and sanitary arrangements were appalling, the drainage being so bad that lavatories were constantly being blocked and the civilian authorities were extremely inefficient. Secondly, all the houses on the opposite side of the street seemed to be brothels – and not particularly hygienic ones at that. It was easy enough to declare them out of bounds, but very difficult to enforce the order. My senior Medical Officer lectured to the men on the dangers of disease but he was worried about it. Shut up in their accommodation after curfew with bad lighting, bad smells and not much to do, these houses opposite presented considerable attractions for many of the airmen, and they were hard to resist.

We even went to the lengths of considering whether we should inspect and approve one or more of these houses, totally against all regulations. In fact most of the men were sensible and responsible, taking good heed of the MO's warning with the result that disease never became a serious problem.

Nevertheless, I remember one unusual incident. An army Military Policeman – a Red Cap – put an airman on a charge and he appeared before me one morning. He was charged with being out after curfew and, on being accosted, failing to produce his identity card and with not wearing his cap. As the

105

charge proceeded, I asked the policeman where the airman was and what he was doing. I received the astonishing reply that he was in a brothel, lying naked on a bed. This was too much and, after further questioning, I had to dismiss the frivolous charge. I then called the policeman back and demanded what on earth he meant by framing such a stupid charge for a serious offence. He looked very embarrassed, hesitated and finally said, 'Well, sir, we get on well with your airmen and I didn't want to get 'im into too much trouble. And, sir, – 'e was enjoying 'imself.' I threw him out while trying to keep a straight face and sent for the airman again. What I said to him need not be repeated but he was left in no doubt that he had escaped a considerable punishment.

One morning the Adjutant, Bill Lawrence came into my office with a small piece of pasteboard in his hand and said, 'There's a gentleman to see you from KLM, the Royal Dutch Airline.'

'Are you sure?' I asked, hardly able to believe my ears. Lawrence handed me the visiting card. Mr Os van Delden, Representative of KLM, it said, with the KLM monogram on top. Lawrence showed him in. He was an extremely smart man of about forty five with smooth black hair and a small moustache. He smiled and we shook hands.

'My company, which I am sure you know well enough, has received permission from the Indonesian government to send a good-will proving flight down our old route from Schipol to Batavia if you are able and willing to accommodate it. I've no doubt you'll be surprised but it has been officially negotiated.'

I was indeed surprised but his request was obviously genuine and put to me pleasantly, almost apologetically, and I liked his manner at once. He said that the aircraft would be a four-engined C54 Skymaster with which KLM had started to equip itself after the War. For some time, he told me, KLM would be dependent along the route to the Far East upon RAF Staging Posts in various countries until, like other airlines, they could set up their own civil organisation at the airfields to be used.

'Of course,' I said, 'we could cope with this proving flight, but have you considered the risks involved in the situation here? I could only give your aircraft the same general protection given to my own and the risk of some form of sabotage is not inconsiderable.'

Privately I was wondering what would be the effects on all of us when the knowledge got out that a Dutch aircraft was allowed into Kemajoran. I could only say, however, that I would have, of course, to clear the matter with my Headquarters as the political implications were considerable. He thoroughly understood my hesitation and thanked me warmly for receiving him. We became good friends during the following months.

The AOC knew of the project but was surprised that van Delden had come to see me so soon. 'It is correct,' he told me, 'that Dr Soekarno has approved a good-will flight and it seems to reveal a ray of hope in the political situation and may help our very delicate negotiations to obtain the release of the more isolated internees. It will also give a great boost to the Dutch nationals who are here and who are very bitter about the conditions, and not too sure about our attitude. As Sorel-Cameron has always said, we are the 'meat in the sandwich' and any gesture of good will we can offer may make our rescue work a little easier.'

This was yet another strange development in the crazy, post-war situation in which we found ourselves; and so Ted Cotton was told to make the best arrangements he could on the airfield for the arrival of the first civil airliner from Holland – indeed, from Europe.

Some time later, the Skymaster – NL300 – duly floated down onto our runway, flown by Captain Parmentier. He was a famous KLM veteran whom I remembered as flying with Captain Moll the Douglas airliner often called the 'Flying Hotel' which had come second in the London to Australia air race of 1934 – second, that is, to the De Havilland Comet.

Parmentier was an immaculate and dapper man of great experience who always flew with gloves on and maintained

107

extremely strict discipline in his aircraft. It had apparently been agreed that he should take the Skymaster up to Bandoeng to visit those of the Dutch community who had not been interned or were now being released. Parmentier invited me to accompany him. I appreciated his gesture but also felt that I should go as a senior officer of the occupying forces.

We had parked the aircraft on the opposite side of the 'out of use' runway to the Dakotas, far enough from the perimeter to be reasonably safe from unwelcome attention. I was invited to take the second pilot's seat and we set off early in the morning. Once in the air, the cockpit was explained to me and I was invited to take the controls and fly the aircraft to Bandoeng, pointing out various features and problems during the flight which took thirty five minutes. Parmentier took over and carried out one of his perfect approaches and landings, commenting on the long line of Japanese Zeros beside the runway. 'They all look in pretty good shape,' I said, 'but we haven't had any instructions about disposing of them.'

There was a tumultuous welcome from the small Dutch crowd and I tactfully left them to it while I inspected our RAPWI Movements cell which was operating from a marquee on the tarmac, processing the next Dakota load of internees waiting to go down to Batavia.

Captain Parmentier and his crew were taken off somewhere or other to breakfast and although I was invited to join the party, I excused myself on the pretext of having business to conduct on the airfield. We returned to Kemajoran two hours later, taking about thirty internees with us. Again I was invited to fly the Skymaster on the return journey. I pointed out the road and the railway where the ambushes had occurred: the wreckage of some of the railway wagons could still be seen. We kept above 3000 feet as there was always the risk of collecting a bullet at low altitude. Two days later the Dutchman departed, taking a full load of internees back to Holland, after expressing the warmest thanks for our help and the work we were doing. Some weeks later, by negotiation, KLM introduced a weekly service from Holland, by which time we were able with the help of van Delden to make more suitable and permanent arrangements for the Skymasters and their crews.

We were now into the early part of December. Heavy banks of cloud were building up each day and one could almost feel the approach of the expected rains. At least the station was now in better shape, slightly more comfortable and operating reasonably efficiently. But it needed to be, as the internal situation around all three British bridgeheads was serious, with the Army meeting fanatical resistance on all fronts as it endeavoured to penetrate towards the inland prison camps, most of which had been identified by RAPWI, but not yet reached.

10

Intensive Operations Continue

The expected rains started in December but fortunately not as heavily as later in the New Year, which was just as well as December turned out to be the busiest month of all on the operational front. As the result of urgent requests to Mr Atkinson in Singapore, he managed to ship to us a large quantity of Pierced Steel Planking (PSP) which we now badly needed, not for any runway use but to make hard standings for the Dakotas and the Air Despatch soldiers who had to load and unload them.

Although the rains turned the top few inches of the grassed areas into a sea of mud, we discovered that the subsoil was rock hard, with the fortunate result that the aircraft did not bog down. Nevertheless, servicing them and taxiing them became a very messy business and there was always some risk that the mud on wheels might prevent undercarriages from being raised and lowered fully. Overlaying the more important parking areas with PSP made a great deal of difference.

Every attempt to extend the three British bridgeheads was met by fanatical Indonesian resistance. Army casualties mounted alarmingly, to such an extent that it was said that 23 Division had more casualties in four months in Java than during a year's hard fighting in Burma. I cannot vouch for the accuracy of this statement but it is sufficient to say that the casualties were extremely high. Troops operating in the Semarang bridgehead, which had been thought to be the safest area, became divided and a powerful air strike by Thunderbolts on targets in the centre of the town was necessary to disperse Indonesian concentrations and permit the troops to join up. Three days later Pat Kennedy led four aircraft of his squadron on a strafing mission between Semarang and Ambarawa when intense and accurate anti-aircraft fire was encountered. It was so good that one wondered whether the weapons were being fired by Japanese. It was an unconfirmed suspicion but, tragically, it resulted in one Thunderbolt being shot down. The aircraft, flown by Flying Officer Crawshay-Fry, plunged into the lake at Ambarawa and disappeared. I was very upset by this incident as only days before I had interviewed and strongly recommended this fine young officer for a permanent commission in the Royal Air Force.

It had become known that several prison camps existed near-by which made it imperative for the Army to press on towards Ambarawa against fierce opposition. On several occasions Ghurka troops became separated from their main force and had to be supported by supply-dropping Dakotas, followed by Thunderbolt attacks on concentrations of Indonesians on the Semarang to Ambarawa road. There were many casualties on both sides during this operation. Several Dakotas were hit during the low level supply drops but none were put out of action. Eventually the main road was cleared and Ambarawa occupied with the subsequent release of 10,000 internees. Unhappily their release was not without cost to them as the

Indonesians turned their attention to the prison camps just as they had done in Bandoeng, and a number of men, women and children were killed and mutilated. It was at once clear that the Army could not advance further without vengeance being wreaked on the hapless prisoners. Patient negotiation was going to be the only way to release the internees from the camps now known to exist further inland.

With the road open and secured, however, it became possible to evacuate those who could be concentrated in Ambarawa to Semarang where they were picked up by Dakotas and flown to Batavia. At least progress was being made but at considerable cost.

Jogjakarta was the capital city of Central Java, situated a long way inland from Ambarawa, and it was known that thousands more internees were being held in camps around that city and also near Soerakarta in the same area. They were both held by the Indonesians and quite unapproachable. Both cities had radio stations which constantly poured out seditious broadcasts. So troublesome were these broadcasts that it was decided to destroy them.

The task was given to the rocket-firing Mosquitos, which effectively silenced Soerakarta, but Jogjakarta, although damaged, still showed life. A second attack, this time by both rocket-firing and bomber Mosquitos, finally silenced the remaining station. The accuracy of all the 904 Wing squadrons was excellent, not only during their attacks but also in locating their targets in poorly mapped country. In view of the number of hits sustained by Dakotas during supply dropping missions in these dangerous areas, they were invariably escorted by fighters which were frequently able to identify and attack gun positions seen to be firing at the Dakotas which were, of course, extremely vulnerable at the low level and slow speed necessary to drop their loads accurately.

I flew a Thunderbolt down to Soerabaya at about this time, with my faithful escort alongside and found that, although operations were not quite as intensive as in the Central region, the Thunderbolts and Mosquitos were actively engaged every day, attacking gun positions, bridges, transport and any other targets detailed by the Army. It was during an early morning reconnaissance flight that a Thunderbolt was hit by extremely accurate anti-aircraft fire and the pilot was compelled to bale out. He was captured but happily was treated quite well and returned to us some months later when the political negotiations became more successful. In the same area, a Mosquito was also shot down but both crew members were killed. These incidents again roused our suspicion that the anti-aircraft guns, in particular, were being operated by the Japanese. It was difficult to believe that Indonesian extremists could have achieved such accuracy with relatively sophisticated weapons in such a short time. It had been estimated that there had been 26,000 Japanese army troops in Java at the time of the capitulation. Very few had been evacuated to Japan by the end of the year: the necessary shipping simply did not exist and internees and released prisoners of war had to be given priority. Inevitably, therefore, thousands of Japanese were still in their units all over the island, and doubtless having a final fling at the Allies. The situation was most unpleasant.

The Wing had been reinforced by two useful aircraft – both Beaufighters from a Jungle Rescue squadron in Malaya. This squadron had done some valuable rescue work in the jungles of Burma and Malaya. There was no specific need for that role in the situation which obtained in Java but, nevertheless, these two aircraft were of inestimable value in dropping warning leaflets of any attack which was likely to result in casualties to innocent civilians, such as the destruction of the two broadcasting stations. We also used them for various reconnaissance missions, as well as for photographing the results of air attacks, thus preserving flying hours of the Mosquitos.

Under cover of our presence a number of Photographic Reconnaissance Spitfires spent some time at Kemajoran to carry out a photographic survey of the island. This was part of an overall policy to survey those areas of South East Asia occupied by the British in order to update maps which, in most cases, were hopelessly inadequate for navigation purposes. These Spitfires worked away quietly at their task for several months, their films being returned to Singapore for processing.

Reports of our successes in the Central and Eastern regions must have filtered through to Batavia because this month of December saw greatly increased hostile activity in the Bandoeng-Batavia area which previously had been thought to be under reasonable control. Far from it. Road convoys had to be heavily escorted and many attacks were made on them from well positioned ambushes. Aircraft were frequently called upon to attack road blocks with gun fire. In one such incident, our Air Contact Team directed Thunderbolts onto a target a mere fifty yards from the convoy with great success, but it was an unnerving experience for both troops on the ground and the pilot himself. It seemed inevitable that a penalty would have to be paid for this dangerous work, and a Mosquito escorting one convoy crashed near the road, both members of the crew being killed. It was never firmly established whether this was an accident or whether the aircraft had been shot down, but the latter seemed the more likely.

Road convoys were continued at irregular intervals, each one being heavily escorted as it was considered important to clear the Bandoeng road; and this was eventually achieved but the cost was high.

In Bandoeng itself, a heavy and very successful air attack had to be launched against a strongpoint lying between the British forces and a large prison camp which was being starved of food and had received no supplies for several days. The strong point was completely destroyed, enabling the Army to render immediate aid to the unfortunate internees who had endured great suffering. I saw many of them a few days later when I took a Thunderbolt up to Bandoeng, taking a cup of terrible coffee with them in the marquee on the tarmac where they were being processed and given a brief medical check before being flown down to Batavia in the next Dakota. They were all in wonderful spirits and so delighted, as well as grateful, to be going back to their homes again. Some were so weak that they burst into tears as they talked but I couldn't help thinking that most of the women had stood up to internment better than the men.

Several more attacks with rockets and bombs had to be made in the Bandoeng area which enabled the Army to clear a large area of extremists and virtually obtain control of the whole city. These attacks were, in fact, the last time in which Kemajoran based aircraft used rockets and bombs. Gun attacks had to be continued for some time on specific targets, notably on the main road which had given us so much trouble, but the worst of the Indonesian resistance in this bridgehead died down.

Nevertheless the battle was not over and a most distressing incident took place – the worst tragedy to befall 904 Wing during its stay in Java. One of our Dakotas was taking Indian reinforcements to Semarang when it had an engine failure and was compelled to turn back. It was heavily loaded with a crew of four RAF personnel and twenty fully armed and equipped Indian soldiers.

The Dakota steadily lost height on its single engine and a Thunderbolt in the area was diverted by the control tower to escort it back to the airfield. It failed to make it and had to carry out a forced landing in a paddy field four miles from the airfield. The wheels-up landing was a good one and the Thunderbolt pilot watched as all the occupants tumbled out and appeared to be uninjured. He radioed the position of the crash to the tower and flew back to report the incident.

A crash party with a strongly armed escort of the RAF Regiment set out at once and had a difficult journey over paddy fields and marshy land before reaching the site of the crash about an hour later. The Dakota was surrounded by a noisy and threatening mob of Indonesians several hundred strong, armed with a variety of weapons. There was no sign of the crew or the passengers and the aircraft was being systematically looted. Unless they opened fire on the mob, there was no way that the crash party could get near to the aircraft and the Regiment officer in charge rightly decided that a pitched battle, with casualties on both sides, would inevitably result and must be avoided. It was observed that a large village, subsequently identified as Bekasi, was situated within a few hundred yards of the crash and the threatening mob clearly came from that village.

The crash party retired from the scene covered by the Regiment detachment, the vehicles making their way back to Kemajoran across the difficult country with a considerable risk of getting bogged down.

By this time the light was fading and a council of war was held with Air Commodore Stevens and the General. It was decided that a whole battalion would approach and occupy Bekasi at first light the following morning in the hope of finding and releasing the crew and passengers. A 904 Wing Air Contact Team would accompany the troops with Thunderbolts overhead in case air support was needed.

Initially none of the Dakota's occupants could be found among the sullen and hostile villagers until an Indonesian woman in a cell in the village gaol said that, from her cell window, she had witnessed the massacre of our men. She then pointed out that they had been buried in a certain area of the river bank. She was unfortunately correct and the mutilated remains of the RAF crew and the twenty Indian soldiers were disinterred and brought back to Batavia. Such was their state that it was almost impossible to identify them although it was clear that there were no survivors. I can hardly describe the horror and fury which this tragedy aroused among us all and there was an immediate call for reprisals with a heavy bombing raid on Bekasi favoured.

General Christison took a very firm line, deciding that the Army would carry out the reprisals and destroy every house in the village which could be identified with the atrocity. Correctly in my view, he forbade the RAF to participate in this operation as he fully understood our feelings and feared that indiscriminate revenge might well be taken if 904 Wing were to be involved. However, we were to cover the operation and photograph the results.

The Army did a thoroughly efficient job on the following day, arresting many young fanatics who were then identified as belonging to a notorious gang known as the 'Black Buffaloes'. A large quantity of weapons was captured and, so involved was the village as a whole that most of it was razed to the ground.

What remained an unsolved mystery about this terrible atrocity was how the fully armed Indian troops in the Dakota did not apparently use their weapons to defend themselves and were somehow lulled into a false sense of security. The Thunderbolt pilot, who was over the crash, was quite adamant that the passengers had all got out of the aircraft safely and, by the time he left to report the incident, there was no sign of hostility towards them. What happened between the departure of the Thunderbolt and the arrival of the crash party can only be a matter of conjecture.

Kemajoran experienced a sense of deep shock for many days and almost everybody on the station attended the funeral of the four members of the RAF crew who were accorded full military honours and buried in our newly consecrated cemetery on the airfield. All flying and work was stopped and a complete silence descended on the station during the service.

It was always easy to be wise after an event and I agonised for a long time about any steps which could have been taken to avoid this tragedy. Should the Thunderbolt have remained over the crash or its place taken by other aircraft while he landed to report the details? If aircraft remained overhead, could they be ordered to open fire if the villagers appeared hostile? Should the Army have been asked to produce a considerable force to accompany the crash party, thereby delaying its arrival at the crash site considerably? None of these questions seemed to me to need an affirmative answer. The crash had occurred within five miles of the airfield in what had hitherto been regarded as a relatively safe area near Batavia. We had no right to open fire on what might have been villagers coming to help. Army reinforcements would have taken time to assemble and it was important that the crash party reached the scene without delay. The Regiment officer in charge was clearly right not to hazard his small crash party in the circumstances. These and other possibilities ran through my mind for a long time but none of them seemed feasible and I was left with the feeling that it was yet another unpleasant manifestation of the predicament in which we found ourselves in Java.

I do not know whether news of this incident alerted the gangs of hostile Indonesians to the firm action which British forces were always prepared to take if their humanitarian work was opposed, but from mid December the situation throughout the island was calmer and very little offensive air action by the Wing was necessary. It may have been that the Indonesian government was beginning to exercise greater control and some restraint upon the hostile gangs as a result of the political negotiations which continued at the highest level. Some proof of this was evident when I was instructed to provide a safe passage for an Indonesian general to land at Kemajoran for high level discussions in the city. It produced a most extraordinary, indeed almost laughable incident. On the day the visiting general, whose name was Subidio, was expected, two small Japanese training aircraft appeared over the airfield. They were single-engined two seater aircraft and, as they appeared to have no radio, they were given permission from the control tower to land, using the green Aldis lamp signal. It was a calm, fine day as the first aircraft came into land, swung off the runway and stood on its nose to the astonishment of those of us who were watching. Before we could do anything about it, the second one charged down the runway, swung off and dug its wing into the ground, coming to a rest in a drunken attitude. I rushed out in my car with the fire tender in hot pursuit, to find General Subidio marooned some fifteen feet above the ground in the first aircraft. We helped him to slide down the fuselage, somewhat shaken and quite unhurt but clearly furious with his pilot. As I had been instructed to treat him with every courtesy, I drove him to my office, gave him a cup of coffee and waited for a government car to collect him. He spoke a little English and was in a towering rage at the indignity of his arrival. All four occupants of the two aircraft disappeared into the city and, in fact, that was the last we ever saw of them.

The next thing I noticed was that the airmen, who were roaring with laughter at this free show, intended to drag the two aircraft away to join the Japanese wreckage at the far side of the airfield. I had to stop this as, for all I knew, it might prejudice the political negotiations. Both aircraft were well clear of the runway and so we left them in position until some decision about their disposal was forthcoming. As far as I could ascertain, Subidio had come from Jogjakarta whence he and his companions must have returned by road as they never appeared either to inspect or collect their broken aircraft. In due course we removed them, taking some care to do no more damage, and there they remained for the rest of our stay. I was half expecting some criticism of our runway or our arrangements for the landing, totally unjustified though it would have been, but the subject never came up again.

I had been feeling for some weeks that I would like to fly the Dakota and participate in some of the work of the squadron. When the matter was raised with Brian Macnamara he fully agreed that I should fly with him initially and get to know the aircraft. We left for Semarang early one morning and I occupied the right hand seat while he ran through the various drills and procedures during the flight. On the return journey, I took the left hand seat and flew back to Kemajoran, carrying out my first Dakota approach and landing under the guidance of my expert tutor. 'Don't attempt to do a three point landing,' said Brian. 'The Dakota likes to be landed on its main wheels with the tail wheel coming down as the speed decreases. A three point landing almost invariably results in a bounce.'

I followed his advice and found that the aircraft landed quite naturally on its two wheels and, if held in that position, the tail came down gently after a short run.

'That was fine: come and fly with us whenever you can.'

'I would like to do a trip at least once a week,' I replied, 'but I think I should always take one of your qualified pilots with me. The passengers you bring back have had a bad enough time without having to be flown out of captivity by an inexperienced Group Captain.'

After this initiation I flew on many sorties with the squadron which were not only enjoyable and released me from the office for an hour or two, but also enabled me to check up on the problems of Bandoeng, Soerabaya and Semarang.

One particular load which we frequently transported was dried fish packed in sacks – apparently part of the staple diet of the Indonesians. It was a horrible load which smelt to high Heaven and, as flakes of the stuff fell down into cracks in the aircraft, it was impossible to get rid of the smell after unloading. The weak and often ill evacuees who came back on the return journeys had to endure the smell, which added to the discomfort, particularly of a rough or bumpy flight. Nevertheless they were so overjoyed at being rescued that they were happy enough to bear the inconvenience, and nobody ever complained – except, of course, the crew, as even the flight deck was not immune from the all-pervading stink. We all learned to hate dried fish.

One of the greatest pleasures of my time in Java was to see and hear the gratitude of the people we brought back as we handed them into the care of the Red Cross. Some of the young children were so thin and emaciated that we sometimes had to strap two of them into their seats with only one seat belt. These passengers were always flown with the greatest consideration at fairly low altitudes and in the smoothest conditions which could be found. This latter consideration was not always easy to achieve as the build-up of cloud during the day, often with heavy rain, tended to make the air rough and bumpy – but the squadron always did its best.

I had one particularly unpleasant flight back from Semarang with a full load of twenty-five evacuees. It was pouring with rain, the clouds were low and the Dakota wallowed about at every level I tried. I flew out to sea, hoping that it might be more comfortable and turned in as we approached Tanjoeng Priok. It was raining heavily over the airfield – almost of monsoon intensity – and the runway was flooded. Consequently, the moment we touched down on our 'mattress', a sheet of water shot up in front of us bringing the Dakota to a halt in a few hundred yards. There was a good deal of sickness on that trip but it was unavoidable. It was the pattern of many flights during the rainy season.

11

Christmas

Owing to the calmer situation in mid December very few air strikes were called for by the Army. But the work of the Dakotas continued unabated, with the daily delivery of supplies within the bridgeheads and the evacuation of prisoners and internees. I had great admiration for all the airmen of the Dakota squadron: their aircraft were much too large to fit into our small hangars and the discomfort of changing an engine, for example, on a platform of PSP in the open amid rain and mud can be imagined. If we could possibly send an aircraft up to Singapore for a major job to be done we did so, but that was the exception, and Brian Macnamara's squadron maintained a high standard of serviceability in spite of all the vicissitudes.

It had not escaped our notice that Christmas was approaching rapidly and I was determined that we would make it as enjoyable and festive as circumstances would permit. Everybody's thoughts were turning to home and wondering how their families would be spending the first Christmas after the war. Many, indeed most, of the airmen who were on 'hostilities only' engagements felt quite understandably that they ought to be at home by this time instead of living rough in mud and heat in a country which really seemed to be no concern of theirs. However, they could see the streams of unfortunate men, women and children being brought out daily from the prison camps and they were loyal and responsible enough to appreciate that our humanitarian job had to be completed. But they grumbled and who could blame them? When Sir Keith Park, the Air Commander-in-Chief, came to address them from Singapore one day, a large chalked notice appeared on the Hangar door 'Roll on that bloody boat.' He could see it, and so could I, but no comment was made by either of us, and a few grinning airmen rubbed it off afterwards.

I formed a small committee of officers and airmen under George Rumsey to work out a programme of Christmas festivities and to deal with the problem of getting in supplies of Christmas fare. The NAAFI had not yet set up shop in Java but was by this time fully established in Singapore. The daily Dakota run brought in NAAFI supplies and we had managed to set up a small shop on the station holding a quantity of essentials which the airmen could buy with sterling.

But these supplies were not adequate for Christmas and so an officer and Warrant Officer were despatched to Singapore with instructions to buy large quantities of everything we would need for the various functions being planned. Included was to be a sack full of toys as we were determined to give the children of Adek camp a party. The NAAFI manager in Singapore was most helpful and large quantities of food and drink were packed, sent out to Kallang airport and loaded on Dakotas over a period of a fortnight. He also selected and sent some one hundred toys for children of various ages. Our problem then became one of storing all these goodies safely, but it was

123

overcome by using part of one of the hangars, with the RAF Regiment keeping an eagle eye on it.

The airmen entered into the spirit of Christmas to the full and even managed to find some way of decorating their houses. It wasn't really practicable to have a competition for the best decorations as they lived in so many small houses, unlike the decorated barrack blocks which used to be such a feature elsewhere in the RAF. Nevertheless, great originality was shown and I paid a visit to all the houses as we ran up to Christmas and had a drink in many of them. The transport section managed to produce a train using a heavily disguised jeep towing three equally disguised bomb trolleys. This turned out to be a huge success with the children who were all given a tour round the aeroplanes. What they really enjoyed was the halt beside the runway to watch aircraft taking off and landing because, of course, flying had to continue throughout the holiday period.

It was decided that the children's party would be on Christmas Eve and we asked Adek to send as many children as they liked with mothers welcome – indeed encouraged – to come with the younger ones. I think we collected sixty-two children and ten mothers in a small fleet of vehicles, to arrive at the airfield at 2 pm.

They were driven straight out to the tarmac to await the arrival of Father Christmas. Fortunately it was a fine, dry day and they lined up in a noisy, excited bunch by the flagstaff. No sleigh or reindeers could be found and so Father Christmas was compelled to fly in by Dakota from some mythical place far away. Promptly at 2.30 his Dakota landed and taxied up to the tarmac with Father Christmas, whom it was said bore a striking resemblance to the Station Commander, waving from the pilot's seat with his long white beard flowing from the open window. I may say that I had changed my flying helmet and earphones for a red and white hat at the end of the runway.

Engines were stopped and Father Christmas emerged from the door with his traditional sack of toys on his shoulder, almost falling down the steps in his Wellington boots and impeded by the weight of his sack. Most of the children were Dutch and had probably never seen a real Father Christmas before. Pandemonium broke loose, and sweating profusely in my heavy disguise, I was engulfed by the cheering, shouting mob. I think the airmen who had turned out to watch this performance enjoyed it as much as the children as I led the way to the airman's dining hall where a big feast had been laid out by our perspiring cooks.

I took up my place in a chair on the platform with a table loaded with presents beside me because my sack had very few in it. As I spoke no Dutch, I wondered how to talk to the children but I needn't have worried. To my astonishment many of them spoke a little English and one of the mothers stood beside me to interpret where necessary and to help me give a suitable present to each child. I didn't want to give a doll to a twelve year old boy and as the presents were wrapped up it needed a little sorting, so two more ladies stood by the table and identified the presents.

Who should walk in during this performance but Air Commodore Stevens and Hughie Edwards, and I insisted on presenting them each with a toy aeroplane. They wandered around chatting to the mothers and the children as well as to the airmen who were looking after the feast of jellies, cakes and lemonade. The airmen helpers, whom I called 'Friends of Adek', had all been visitors to the camp during the past two months and made many friends there.

'If I don't get out of this rig soon, I shall pass out,' I muttered to George Rumsey. 'Why did I let myself in for this?' When tea was at last over, it was time for rides on the train, twenty at a time, driven by a fearsome looking engine driver, who was quite unrecognisable. This was the cue for Father Christmas to leave. This I did with the first train load of children to the far side of the airfield where I said goodbye and walked off into the distance with my empty sack: my car was waiting behind some tents by the bomb dump, and I couldn't get out of my disguise quickly enough. Within ten minutes I was back in the Mess with a cold beer. The children went off at 5 o'clock to beat the curfew, cheering wildly as they drove out of the gates. It had been a great success.

The next day was Christmas Day and we made as much of a holiday of it as possible subject to the needs of operational readiness and security. All our thoughts turned to home as the chaplain held a big open air service and made remembrance of our loved ones the theme of his address. There must have been a thousand airmen at that service which was held close to the newly consecrated cemetery where already a dozen members of 904 Wing were buried and remembered during the service. I wondered how many more there would be before this unpleasant extension of the war came to an end. As I finished reading the lesson and looked up over those hundreds of scruffy but splendid airmen standing quietly in the shimmering heat, the full realisation of our isolation from all we knew and loved hit me very hard. The men dispersed very quietly, each one doubtless occupied with his own thoughts.

In true RAF tradition, the airmen's Christmas dinner was served by the officers. The cooks had done a splendid job, the only thing missing from the menu being turkey, which was quite unobtainable. Chickens, which had led a pretty active life, were the only available substitute but with all the trimmings they were quite acceptable.

A swimming party had been arranged for the afternoon for those who could manage to stay awake and away from the lure of their 'charpoys' (beds). We found it reasonably safe to drive to a beach beyond the docks at Tanjoeng Priok, but two airmen with rifles always remained on guard while the troops swam. A delightful, golden beach was backed by coconut palms and a few small boys from a nearby village were always on hand to swarm up the trees and throw coconuts down for a bar of chocolate. The villagers here were very shy but perfectly friendly and always watched the antics of the swimmers from a distance. In a small way this did a lot of good for relations and we never had the slightest trouble from that particular village.

126

The swimming here was magnificent with the clearest blue water and sand and coral below. As a precaution, a medical orderly with a small pack-up was usually included in each party but his expertise was seldom needed.

The curfew was still in force this Christmas which greatly restricted any entertainment which the city might offer after dark, but we had managed by this time to set up an open air cinema with a reasonable supply of films from Singapore, allowing about three different showings per week. I can't remember what it was, but a good film had been reserved for Christmas night after a football team of airmen had given the officers and warrant officers a terrible thrashing by seven goals to one – the one being an own goal!

Now it was time for the officers to have their own Christmas dinner. Several of them had come to me and said that they would like to make it a formal dining-in night, and would I kindly write out the drill for such occasions. It hadn't previously occurred to me that I was the only regular officer in the Wing Headquarters. The practice of dining-in Mess had not, for obvious reasons, been carried on during the war in South East Asia and I do not think at this time it had been generally restarted. We had, of course, no Mess kit and could only dine in our best jungle green or khaki drill.

I was pleased at this proposal and spent a little time recalling the etiquette, starting with everyone seeking out the senior officer present when he entered the Mess and saying 'Good evening, Sir' to him.

I then detailed a President and Vice-President and outlined the procedure for the loyal toast and passing of the port which, incidentally, we had obtained from the NAAFI. Ladies names were not to be mentioned nor rude jokes told before the loyal toast, nor was smoking allowed until the port circulated. Anybody wishing to leave the table had to walk up and seek President's permission, thus drawing attention to himself. I omitted the old fashioned rule of no smoking and sherry only before dinner: that seemed to be carrying formality too far in these enlightened days.

Twenty-two sat down to dinner, all smartly dressed in bush jackets and slacks in our small hotel dining room and consulted the most extraordinary menu, a copy of which I have retained. It had been tastefully illustrated with Javanese dancing girls to distract attention from the basically compo ration menu which read as follows:-

Potage crème de tomate
Poisson Batavia
Porc rôti. Poulet coriace garni
Sauce nature

Wot! No Turkey!
Quoi! Pas de dindon!

Pommes de terre sautées,
Purée de patate,
Petits pois durs.
Choux de Chine à choix.
Pouding Noël à la crème Martel.
Compote de Fruits de Java au gâteau.
Tartelettes de Noël à l'anglais.
Fromage cartonné très vieux.
Biscuits. Dessert. Café

I have reproduced this menu exactly as written and take no responsibility for some of its oddities. Every officer signed the copy which I have and one had written, 'Wot a Wing – I like it.' Morale could not have been all that bad!

We had, of course, no band to accompany our dinner and so, in lieu of a bandmaster coming to take a glass of port with the President as custom dictated, we invited our two cooks to do likewise. They had done wonders in their primitive kitchen with the doubtful assistance of compo rations. Fortunately our dependence on these very basic commodities was decreasing as local traders gradually became more friendly and co-operative although the problem of an acceptable currency had not yet been fully resolved.

These Christmas festivities were not marred by any casualties or serious incidents within the Wing and there was some indication that the Indonesian government was slowly gaining a greater measure of control over the extremists. The Prime Minister, Sjahrir, was making great efforts to calm the situation and, had it not been for the intransigence of certain Dutch personnel and the bitter hatred of the Indonesian for the Dutch, his efforts would have undoubtedly achieved quicker results. Nevertheless the tide was gradually turning and the prospects for 1946 looked considerably brighter. One unpleasant incident only affected us shortly after Christmas. Two shots from either a rifle or revolver were fired from the darkness of the main road into the verandah of our Officers' Mess. They ploughed into the woodwork and nobody was hit in spite of the fact that the verandah, which did duty as our sitting room, was lighted and occupied by several officers. A car was heard speeding away and the culprits were not caught but it created a problem as the verandah was the only place to sit and it was not feasible to have lights out and metal screens, but the security of our sitting room remained a constant source of concern.

The year came to an end fairly quietly. The curfew could not yet be lifted but great strides were being made by the Army to round up the extremists in the city and free it from all too frequent attacks on individuals and property. What was needed now was speedier results from the negotiations to enable us to free the thousands of internees still incarcerated in camps far inland.

12

Disaffection

During the first few days of 1946, disturbing rumours began to reach Batavia through passengers and aircrew arriving daily by the scheduled Dakota from Singapore.

It was said that numbers of airmen at RAF stations in India and Ceylon had refused to obey their officers' orders and had gone 'on strike'. To begin with I did not understand this. Airmen were on active service in South East Asia and refusal to obey orders would normally be regarded as mutinous, for which the punishment was exceedingly severe. It transpired later, however, that higher authority decreed that these occurrences were to be called 'strikes' which, in the circumstances, was probably a wise move.

As the days passed the rumours hardened into firm reports. It appeared that the airmen concerned in these incidents were led by the few troublemakers to be found in any community, and their grievances were concerned with what they regarded as the slow rate of repatriation and demobilisation. Some were angry at having been sent to the Far East after the victory in Europe, while others had already completed long tours in acute discomfort in Burma.

A sound enough scheme was in existence for repatriation, but it was lagging behind schedule owing to the critical shortage of shipping and transport aircraft resulting from the losses incurred during the war.

These reasons did not appeal to many of the airmen who had insufficient work to occupy them in India, Malaya and Singapore, and the seeds of discontent were sown. It was easy enough to lay the blame upon poor officer leadership, a view which some senior officers held, but it has to be remembered that only about 10% of the more junior officers at that time were regulars. The remaining 90% were on 'hostilities only' commissions and had received virtually no training in leadership during the war years. Like the disgruntled airmen, many of these were overdue for repatriation, had families waiting for them at home and were worried about their prospects for finding civilian employment.

Such excuses cannot, and could not, be accepted for the breakdown in discipline which we were beginning to hear about. 904 Wing was stuck out on a limb hundreds of miles ahead of the main RAF force in South East Asia, extremely busy with a difficult and often dangerous and unpleasant task to perform. Consequently there was great concern as to whether these reports and rumours, some of them considerably exaggerated, would begin to infect our own airmen. The Royal Air Force had never in its history experienced this kind of disaffection and it was clearly a severe and humiliating blow to the prestige of the Service.

By the end of January, there were indications that some officers in Command Headquarters in Singapore were getting jittery and I started to receive frequent telegrams to address the airmen personally on this, that and the other aspects of repatriation, demobilisation and the effect of the strikes in other parts of the Command.

Nothing is more calculated to make an airman feel that his officers are worried than to be called together and addressed at unusually frequent intervals. I felt that the Wing and its squadrons knew the importance of our task and were working hard and conscientiously to carry it out. I had a long talk with Air Commodore Stevens and he fully supported me in my decision to ignore much of the advice coming from Singapore but to pass suitable material to my officers and NCOs with instructions to use it appropriately in their relations with their own airmen and report any signs of disaffection.

Nevertheless, there was real cause for concern and I decided to pay a quick visit to Singapore and find out more about the situation, particularly from my fellow Station Commanders there. With our daily Dakota service there was no need for me to be away for more than two days and so I sent a signal to Charles Reilly, the Station Commander at Kallang, asking him if I could spend a night with him to discuss the problem of disaffection. Although I had never met him I received a welcoming reply.

Brian Macnamara suggested that I should fly the scheduled service Dakota with Flying Officer Brown as co-pilot which would give me experience of a longer flight than I had so far been doing. I took off at 7 am two days later with a passenger list of ten lucky airmen whose release dates had arrived and who were on their way home – in very cheerful mood. There were also eight internees who were equally happy on the first stage of their journey to Holland. There was no smell of dried fish in this aircraft and I suspected that the squadron reserved certain clean Dakotas for this daily run.

It was an enjoyable flight at 8000 feet, high enough to escape the heat and below a level at which oxygen might be needed by some of the passengers, a few of whom looked extremely frail. There are said to be a thousand islands between Java and Singapore, mostly uninhabited, and some of them looked idyllic

132

in the sunshine. I decided that I must do something about setting up that holiday camp island for the troops as soon as I returned.

Three-and-three-quarter hours later, Singapore came in sight and I circled over the city and the harbour which was crowded with shipping. The city had changed little since I last saw it in 1936 but one or two skyscrapers, including the Cathay building, had been added. Although Kallang was at that time a RAF station, it also did duty as the civil airport. It had a single runway covered with PSP which shone in the sunlight. Brown had explained to me that a low stone wall bordered one end of the runway, separating it from the harbour while the other end terminated abruptly at a main road.

'Have you ever landed on PSP?' asked Brown. I shook my head. 'Well don't be alarmed at the crashing and banging when you touch down: the metal surface twists and buckles and we have had the odd puncture here.'

I had been warned, but as the wheels touched after a good approach and landing, I was quite alarmed at the rattling and general metallic uproar which followed. It sounded as if the Dakota had fallen to pieces under me and I instinctively gripped the control column more firmly while Brown grinned beside me.

'If that was a good landing, I wonder what a bad one feels like,' I said as we rattled to a stop.

'No idea, sir, I've never done a bad one, but thank heavens we don't have this stuff at Kemajoran.'

I certainly agreed and blessed Mr Atkinson for providing our mattress-like 'bit hess' surface while I taxied up to the control tower with much clanking from the undercarriage.

Charles Reilly was on the tarmac to meet me and we went to his office for a cup of coffee and a chat. He impressed me as being a very resilient person who was more angry than worried about the disaffection that had spread from India down through Burma to the Singapore stations.

'Before we go across to my bungalow,' he said, 'I ought to tell you that I have the ex-Station Commander from another station

133

staying with me. I say 'ex' because he has just been dismissed from his station for apparently failing to control certain incidents of insubordination. Understandably he is most upset and, from what I hear, his dismissal seems pretty unreasonable. There it is, however, and he is staying with me awaiting a passage home.'

I asked him whether he had had any trouble at Kallang and he replied that there were mutterings and grumbling but so far no flagrant incidents of insubordination, but he and his officers were keeping an extremely close eye on the situation. None of this was in the least comforting and, for the first time, I was rather thankful that my Wing was stuck out in front of the main part of the Command by several hundred miles, and therefore removed from the immediate influence of the trouble makers. Nevertheless there was no reason for complacency.

Reilly lived in a very pleasant, but small bungalow almost on the beach close to his station, and, after a very good dinner, in which compo rations played no part, the three of us settled down on the verandah overlooking the sea for a long discussion. It was a beautiful evening and, as the sun went down, the arc lamps of the fishermen at the end of the bamboo piers which they built out into the sea, began to shine brightly to attract the fish into their nets. The heat died down and a cool breeze came in off the Johore Strait.

At my invitation Charles Reilly spoke of the events in India and elsewhere as he understood them. Apparently the dissatisfaction over the delays in the repatriation programme was influenced by broadcasts by the American service which was widely listened to in South East Asia. These broadcasts reported that US forces in Germany were holding mass parades to demand speedier demobilisation. The publicity given to these demonstrations had a harmful effect on RAF personnel and gave an opportunity to trouble-makers and 'barrack room lawyers' to encourage our airmen to follow the American example.

The first incident erupted in Karachi and, within a few days, spread to RAF stations in Ceylon where airmen refused to service aircraft and carry out other duties. On the whole the airmen were well behaved and respectful to their officers, but adamant that their complaints should be handled expeditiously. This was not easy as little could be done to rectify their demands locally and reference to Air Ministry and the Government at home was essential.

Far from signalling the end of the disturbances, those in Ceylon were but the introduction. They spread throughout India with stoppages of work in Delhi, Calcutta and many other stations in North East India. They were generally of short duration, respectful but determined.

From India the trouble spread rapidly to Singapore and Sir Keith Park himself addressed a mass meeting at Seleter, but the most vocal agitators refused to accept the Air Ministry facts and figures on release. These particular airmen were mostly those who had been sent to the Far East after the capitulation of Japan and were deeply resentful.

Charles Reilly was understandably concerned about his own station, Kallang, and he had every right to be as shortly after I left on the following day he caught an airman red-handed addressing the troops and inciting them to 'come out on strike'. The airman was arrested, court martialled and given ten years imprisonment which was subsequently reduced, and further reduced to a nominal period when he reached home – a very unsatisfactory outcome for such a flagrant breach of discipline.

I now knew exactly what had happened to date, and it confirmed most of the rumours and reports which had reached me in Java. We discussed the problem far into the night. 'Although you are having a rough time in Java,' Reilly said, 'I think you are at least fortunate to be extremely busy doing your Red Cross work and that may save you from trouble. So many of our men here do not have enough worthwhile work to occupy them and that breeds dissatisfaction.'

He went on to tell me that the Inspector-General of the RAF was in the middle of a tour of the Command, and having a fairly rough time on the various stations he was visiting. He was expecting to come to Java in due course but the feeling was that he could do little or nothing to satisfy the men's demands as the speed of the repatriation programme was entirely dictated by the shipping and transport aircraft available.

Charles had done little to comfort me but I was extremely grateful to him for giving me such a full account of events. Early next morning I clattered down his runway in the Dakota and set off back to my own outpost. On this occasion we carried mostly freight but there were also six airmen, newly posted to 904 Wing from home. After an hour I handed over to Brown and went back into the cabin to chat to the passengers and tell them something about Java. They were all regular airmen and seemed pleased to be coming to an operational station, having heard something of our activities while waiting in Singapore. They had not enjoyed their few days in the transit camp while waiting for their flight and were anxious to get down to a job of work.

We ran into cloud and heavy rain after two hours which caused the heavily laden Dakota to wallow about in spite of Brown's efforts to find a smoother height. I got the impression that the monsoon had extended further south than usual this year and we were getting the tail end of it before petering out towards Australia. Conditions improved as we approached Batavia and I left it to Brown to bring us in to a smooth landing, very different from that at Kallang.

A signal was waiting for me, announcing a visit by the Inspector-General in a week's time. This came as no surprise after what I had learned in Singapore but I had already made up my mind that I would prefer him not to address the airmen in a body if I could find some other way in which he could meet and talk to individuals. I felt that he might well be expecting the same sort of problems which he had encountered on stations in India whereas the atmosphere at Kemajoran was quite different.

I called the squadron commanders and my senior officers to a meeting in our Mess that evening, told them what I had learned in Singapore and then discussed how we should handle the visit by Air Chief Marshal Sir Arthur Barratt. They were unanimous in saying that they had no serious problems in their squadrons and units and that they would prefer to show the Inspector-General round and avoid an address to a mass of airmen taken from their work to stand for half an hour in the heat of the day. We would then reserve an hour during which the I-G could interview any airman who wished to have a private and personal talk with him.

'He will be staying with the Air Commodore,' I told them, 'and I have been invited to dinner that night which will be another opportunity to get the latest information about the repatriation programme.'

Two days later I talked to the airmen in the dining hall after their lunch, giving them all the news I had about release and the repatriation programme which was at last beginning to speed up. Coming to the I-G's visit, I told them that they would be able to meet him in their places of work, but if any of them would like an interview with him, they could give their names to the Adjutant and nobody else would be present at the interview. Finally, I asked if anybody had questions for me at this moment.

I had taken the precaution of going to the back of the hall and turning them round to face me, knowing full well that, if there were any difficult customers, they would now be in front and not in the background. There were a few straightforward questions but one airman was very persistent and fired off a string of questions. I could see that most of the men were getting restless with this barrage from the airman and so I brought the meeting to a close saying, 'Your questions are too long and complicated to answer properly here. Perhaps you will come and see me later and I will endeavour to give you the information you want.'

Next morning the airman, who worked in the accounts section, was ushered into my office by the Adjutant, whom I had instructed to remain during the interview. He was a smart airman, immaculately dressed and I had already found out that he was extremely good at his job.

'Well,' I said, 'we all have problems here but you seem to have more than most. Tell me about them.'

He then gave the game away by telling me, not without some pride, that he had been largely responsible for the 'strike' at a certain station in India which had resulted in that station being closed down, and he had been posted to 904 Wing. I could hardly contain my fury as no mention or indication of this had ever been given to us. He was a ring-leader who had obviously been posted as far away as possible to what was probably regarded as a tough spot. That, however, was a matter to be dealt with later. In the meantime something had to be done about this airman. I listened with as much patience as possible to all his complaints about the standard of accommodation and food, the slowness of release and many other shortcomings, of which I was only too well aware.

During this catalogue of complaints, an idea had been germinating in my mind as to how to deal with this man. I looked him in the eye and said, 'Do you know the *real* job of work we are doing here?'

'Well, sir,' he replied, 'I don't see much of it but I know we are bombing and shooting at Indonesians and also ferrying food into the interior.'

'Do you see any of the people we are rescuing from prison camps?'

'No,' he replied, 'I am too busy with the pay ledgers and accounts.'

'Which,' I said, 'I know you do very well, but I'm going to give you the opportunity to see and take part in the real work of the Wing. Every airman, whatever his trade, must be prepared to fly if required to do so and you are going to fly with the Dakota squadron and see exactly who they bring out of captivity.'

'Well,' he muttered doubtfully, 'I'm very busy and that isn't part of my job. In any case, I don't know whether I'm fit enough.'

'How did you get out here?'

138

'I flew, sir, but that's a bit different.'

'If you are fit enough to fly 9000 miles to Java, you are quite fit enough to fly as a passenger in a Dakota for a couple of hours. Anyway, that's an order and you will fly tomorrow. Finally, if I catch you or have reports that you are inciting your colleagues to insubordination, you'll be court martialled. Is that absolutely clear?'

He left without comment and a smart salute. I sent for Brian Macnamara and explained what I wanted to him.

'Take him yourself, Brian; make him sit in the cabin. I particularly want him to see a good load of internees on the return journey so that he can see how frail they are and the suffering they have had to endure.'

The flight took place – complete with dried fish – to Semarang; and a full load of twenty five internees came back, including two on stretchers. I did not wish to see the airman again but asked the Accountant officer about his reactions. He had returned, looking a little green and extremely quiet, getting on with his work without comment. He gave no further trouble and was eventually repatriated when his release date came up about three months later.

I did, however, take the precaution of calling my Warrant Officers and senior NCOs together, not only to explain to them what had happened and to tell them that, as they were closer to the airmen than the officers could possibly be, I wanted them to keep a particularly close eye open for any signs of incitement to insubordination and nip it in the bud. I said that I did not expect any further trouble from that particular airman, but among more than two thousand there was always likely to be the odd trouble-maker who, as I had learned in Singapore, could have a startling effect on his fellow airmen under the conditions in which we were living and working. There were one or two unrepeatable comments about our miscreant but also an assurance that no sign of serious trouble was apparent throughout the Wing.

Sir Arthur Barratt, the Inspector-General, duly arrived in the C-in-C's Dakota looking, I thought, very tired, as we were the last station of a long and exhausting tour. Dinner that night at the Air Commodore's villa in the city, in company with Hughie Edwards and Sorel-Cameron was interesting. A good deal more had been made of the disaffection in India than was strictly justified. Nevertheless, as the I-G said, the incidents had been most embarrassing for the RAF as a whole. Nothing like it had ever happened before and he put it down mainly to the inexperience and lack of leadership by many wartime officers. I felt that this was a little unfair and I think the others present agreed with me. The anti-climax resulting from the sudden end to the war and the unavoidable tardiness of the release programme had left thousands of men stranded in South East Asia without sufficient satisfying work to occupy them. These factors seemed to me to have provided the inflammable material with a few hardened trouble makers providing the spark.

The conversation then turned to the situation in Java. I felt that the I-G expected to find the same problems as he had experienced in India and Singapore, but was clearly relieved when both the Air Commodore and I explained that our airmen understood the humanitarian task on which we were engaged and that understanding, coupled with anger at the waste of life being experienced, seemed to have imbued them with a determination to work hard and finish the job as quickly as possible. What we now needed above all else was success in the political negotiations to allow us to get into the interior of the island and release the last of the prisoners. I said I thought he would see this attitude if he would tour round the Wing next day and talk to airmen in their places of work. Only three airmen had asked to see him personally as a result of my earlier invitation, and I hoped he would listen sympathetically. 'Well,' he said, 'it is a relief to hear this as I haven't enjoyed my tour and have found it most difficult to give satisfying answers to many of the questions I've been asked.'

On the following day Sir Arthur's tour went off well. With my car and driver, he started with Brian Macnamara's Dakota squadron, watched an incoming load of internees, and then moved on to the Thunderbolt and Mosquito squadrons, being handed on from one Commanding Officer to the next until he had visited most of the units and sections on the station.

He arrived back in my office looking pretty hot and weary but a cold drink of fresh lime juice put him to rights again and I left him interviewing the three airmen who had asked to see him. We then went to my own Mess for lunch where he met and chatted to the Wing officers.

'There is no doubt,' he said during lunch, 'that this is an unpleasant extension of the war, but General Christison has told me that his negotiations with Soerkano are bearing fruit and it should be possible to get into the interior prison camps quite soon. I find the spirit and determination here much better than I expected, but we really must not stay in the East Indies a day longer than is necessary to release the internees. The repatriation programme,' he continued, 'is at last speeding up as more shipping becomes available and that should do a lot to improve morale. I have thanked the airmen to whom I spoke this morning for what they are doing and will certainly report it fully when I get home.'

Before the Air Marshal departed in his VIP Dakota the following morning he walked up the tarmac with me and after watching a pair of Thunderbolts tear down the runway and climb away towards Bandoeng said, 'I don't think you have much to worry about. The men seem fully aware of the importance of the job they are doing. They don't like it of course, but the casualties you have suffered – nineteen to date I understand – have made them determined to see this thing through. I shall report the situation here fully when I get back to London next week and do my utmost to get the Government to shorten the tour out here and speed up the repatriation programme.' He climbed into his aircraft with a wave and departed.

In retrospect his visit had been useful, if only to dispel some of the anxieties I had felt since returning from the rather depressing visit to Singapore. Things could only get better and, indeed, the

New Year did bring many improvements which all helped to make life at Kemajoran more comfortable – or should I say less *un*comfortable?

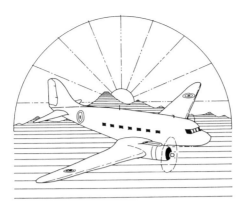

13

Life in Batavia Improves

Until the end of 1945, life for all of us in Batavia had been extremely uncomfortable and restricted, with a constant danger of being shot at by unidentifiable snipers who had mingled with the crowds in the city. Had there not been a curfew the dangers would have been infinitely greater. Even in daytime it was essential for the airmen to move about in pairs, or in greater numbers if possible, and preferably in vehicles rather than on foot.

By the end of January, 1946, however, the Army, now considerably strengthened with many more military police, had rounded up many of the gangs who had terrorised the city in the early days of our occupation. They had done an outstanding job and Batavia was rapidly returning to normal. It had become clear to most of the Indonesian population that our forces had no intention of trying to oust their new government and the deep suspicion which our presence originally aroused died down. The Javanese were simple, peace-loving and friendly people who, once they realised that some form of colonial rule was not going to be re-imposed, warmed to our troops and became much more helpful.

It was also apparent that the political negotiations were making progress and beginning to ease our efforts to get internees out of the more difficult areas although some of the camps deep in the interior still remained unapproachable. In order to facilitate these negotiations, I had two or three small twin-engined Japanese aircraft, still being flown by their Japanese crews. This policy may sound very odd, and indeed it was, but it had its purpose. The flights of these communications aircraft were controlled by the RAPWI staff and were able to take Government and RAPWI officials into areas where our RAF aircraft could not penetrate. They would take off in the morning and disappear: none of us having any idea where they went. It was no real concern of mine as long as they complied with our airfield rules, which they did meticulously. Indeed, so meticulous were they that, as they taxied along the tarmac towards the runway and passed my office, a hatch would open in the cockpit roof and a small helmeted head would pop out and salute smartly. My office was situated immediately behind the flagstaff and I was never quite sure whether they were paying the compliment to me or to the RAF flag! It was amusing and certainly not something to be discouraged. If this daily performance happened to coincide with Miep dishing out 'char and wads' from her truck, the crowd of airmen would invariably raise a loud cheer – doubtless an ironical one.

In addition to our problems of getting the internees out of their camps, had been those of getting them away from Java once released. We couldn't possibly fly them all to Singapore and shipping was scarce. This problem was eased greatly in the New Year when two large Dutch liners arrived from Holland. One was the *Oranje*, a famous Dutch cruising liner in pre-war days, and a sister ship. This other ship was also of 20,000 tons and, when I saw her at Tanjoeng Priok, I could not help thinking that she had to be large to get the whole of her name along the side of the ship. Believe it or not, her name was *Johan van Oldenbarnevelt*. I had some difficulty in remembering this tongue twister which stretched all the way from the bow to the bridge.

Brian Macnamara and two of my other officers went on board with me before she sailed. It was quite an emotional experience as she was filled to capacity, not only with male passengers whom we had evacuated from the camps, but also with a number of women from Adek camp whom we had got to know. Some of them had been re-united with husbands while others were unattached, all thrilled and happy to be on one of their own ships again. The Captain was a rubicund and jolly Dutchman: he gave us a small party at which quantities of Bols gin were drunk before we said goodbye to so many who had passed through our hands. Brian Macnamara, in particular, was sincerely thanked for flying them safely out and ending their terrible privations. That visit, almost more than anything else, made me feel that we were at last making good progress with our primary job in Java.

Those women who still remained in Adek were slowly being taken out and accommodated in a number of hotels which had re-opened for the first time since the occupation. Foremost among these was the Hotel des Indes, the best and most luxurious in the city. Its furnishing and decor had suffered some damage but it was trying hard to regain its old style. Several of the accommodation blocks were reserved for the released internees and we were soon able to close Adek.

Shortly after the hotel opened I went there for lunch with van Delden, the KLM manager with whom I had become very friendly as the result of his frequent visits to Kemajoran to meet the weekly Skymaster from Amsterdam. We had given the airline a PSP hard standing and made the reception as comfortable as we could. My own Servicing Commando handled

145

the refuelling and any servicing needed until KLM produced its own staff later on in the year.

The Hotel des Indes resumed serving its world famous curry luncheon in the huge covered, but otherwise open dining room. This meal intrigued me, having taken a great liking to curry during my previous years in India when you either had to enjoy curry or starve! The hotel served it in great style and the sambals, which I have always considered an essential part of curry, were brought round by a crocodile of no less than thirty-seven small boys, each smartly dressed in a uniform topped by a red fez, and each carrying a different ingredient. This crocodile wound its way between the tables, and one had to be extremely selective to avoid amassing a quite unmanageable load on one's plate.

This was the occasion when van Delden introduced me to Bols gin, regarded by the Dutch as an essential aperitif to curry, or their renowned 'reistaffel'. Initially I did not like it much with its slightly paraffin-like taste, but it improved after the first couple and, as with curry, I acquired the taste. With the hotel curry and several Bols, the glaring Java sun after lunch required sun glasses. After this introduction, I had many curry lunches on a Sunday at the hotel, and equally as many glasses of Bols.

Probably the greatest improvement in conditions came with the lifting of the curfew at about this time. Certain of the less salubrious parts of this teeming city of over a million people were placed out of bounds to all British troops and they were still required to move about after dark in pairs. Such restrictions were essential as isolated incidents of shooting and mugging continued. Indeed, a fusillade of shots broke out close to the Hotel des Indes on one occasion when I was there. It appeared to come from another hotel further up the road and police were immediately on the scene. It was better not to look into the cause of these incidents unless one's men were involved, but they served as a warning to stick to the main thoroughfares and places of entertainment.

146

One of the latter was the Box Club. In pre-war days it had been a European club on the outskirts of the city but it had been closed down and allowed to degenerate during the occupation. The Army asked us to help in rehabilitating it as an Officers' club and try to get some cricket going on the large sports field attached to it. A young Captain in the Seaforth Highlanders took charge of the work and, within a very few weeks, had cleaned up and stocked the clubhouse as well as getting the sports field cut and rolled.

We celebrated on a Sunday with a cricket match between the Army and the RAF. It was a limited-over game starting at 11 am and, most fortunately, was blessed with good weather. Hughie Edwards captained the RAF team and, winning the toss, elected to bat first, not always a wise tactic in limited-over cricket. Hughie, with his Australian background, was a good batsman with quite a lot of experience behind him.

The pitch was pretty rough in spite of the rolling it had received. With thirty five runs on the board, a nasty bouncer glanced off the handle of Hughie's bat and that was the end of him. We soldiered on. I made an inglorious eight runs and the side was eventually all out just after lunch for 105 runs with six overs still to go. I have to admit that the Army team was better than ours and knocked off the necessary runs with three wickets to spare. I made some amends for my poor showing as a batsman by taking two wickets. Unlike present day bowlers, I bowled at the wickets and both of my successes were middle stump affairs.

One of the more amusing aspects of this match was the dress of the players. Of course, nobody had any cricketing gear with them in Java, but gallant efforts were made to appear in 'whites' of some kind. Bats and pads presented no problem and a few old and moth-eaten pre-war relics had been unearthed in the Box Club. Both teams shared the same gear and the game was almost brought to an end when a mighty slog by one soldier resulted in one of our four bats flying into pieces – riddled with wood-worm! The two balls we found were certainly not round, but as

147

the pitch was so rough anyway, that didn't matter much.

At the end of the match a somewhat battered trophy which had also been found in the club was presented to the Army team by the General who then declared the Box Club formally open. That evening the Seaforths produced a dance band to everybody's surprise and, although not many ladies were present, an enjoyable evening made us all feel that the clouds really were beginning to lift over Batavia.

There were other social developments, starting with the expected arrival of NAAFI in the island and within a few days a well stocked shop and a club for soldiers and airmen was started in the centre and safer part of the city. At the same time the issue of Japanese money was stopped as apparently the Netherlands had agreed to meet the cost of the free issues which had been in operation for some three months. Shopkeepers, bars and the club began to accept other currencies, either Malay dollars or Sterling and the halcyon days when the troops, indeed all of us, could save seventy five per cent of our pay were over. We had had a good run for our Japanese guilders which had seen us through the roughest part of the tour and which must have been unique for an occupation force, particularly as we were not called upon to repay the sums issued. My Accountant officer was still left with thousands of these guilders which then had to be destroyed and so lifted a considerable burden from his shoulders.

With the arrival of the NAAFI came our first ENSA concert led by the comedian Tommy Trinder. The curfew had made it impossible to have any form of evening entertainment previously. The ENSA party took over the main theatre and performed every night for a week to packed houses. Trinder was supported by a good troupe of dancing girls – very good judging by the applause – and several excellent solo performers who, in spite of the heat, worked away tirelessly to entertain us. On the last night I drove Tommy Trinder back to our Mess in a jeep with a couple of armed Regiment airmen in the back. There was still some small risk at night for us and several hundred airmen came to see the girls off in a Dakota the following morning.

With the station running as smoothly as it was ever likely to run in the chaos surrounding us, I turned my attention to what I called my 'Treasure Island Project' as the only local leave centre we were ever likely to find. The correct name of the offshore island was Edam but we never referred to it as anything other than Eden island.

A close examination from the air followed by a boat trip seemed to be the first step and so, early one bright sunny morning I climbed into the Wing Thunderbolt after explaining to the control tower where I was going. I waited for a Dakota to land and set off down the runway. At the correct engine speed I pressed the water injection switch and felt the comforting thrust in the back as she lifted off the runway very quickly, having no load on.

It was a beautiful morning, the previous day's heavy rain having washed the sky clean as I circled round the city at 3000 feet, partly in case I had to land again unexpectedly and partly to pursue our policy of letting the population see as many aeroplanes as possible. Turning away and over the docks which were now crowded with shipping, I flew towards Eden island and dropped down to 1000 feet, drew back my canopy and flew round the island at 150 mph with the turbo supercharger grumbling to itself behind my head, a sound which I now found comforting and cheerful.

Golden sand and deep blue water surrounded the island, the centre being covered with scrub and coconut palms. There was no sign of life and I had as close a look at the buildings as a Thunderbolt at 150 mph would permit. The top of the old lighthouse had long since disappeared but about six buildings existed, mostly roofless but brick built and fairly solid. The rotting remains of a small jetty had a path leading up to the buildings. It all looked quite promising and, as I pulled up to about 4000 feet, I decided that a reconnaissance by boat must be the next step with a few technical advisers. Fresh water, for instance, looked as if it might be one of the problems although, if the lighthouse men of old solved it, I was sure the RAF could find a solution. I flew on down the coast for twenty minutes or so before turning back to Kemajoran and receiving the tower's instructions to land behind a Mosquito which I could see dropping down in front of me. As I taxied slowly in, Miep was dishing out her usual elevenses outside the larger of the two hangars and I walked over to have a word or two with the airmen who were treating her to the usual cheerful comments about the quality of her tea. I accepted Flight Sergeant Williams' mug and had a brew myself.

'Look what it's done to my chest,' said one airman whose bare chest was covered with a mass of black hair. I must admit the tea was pretty powerful but Miep had clearly got quite used to these quips and went quietly on with her job. At that moment the Sergeant who looked after my Thunderbolt, and knew where I had been, came up with something in his hand.

'Where have you been, sir? You've got some seaweed on the tail wheel,' holding up what was undoubtedly a large length of seaweed.

'Come off it, Sergeant,' I said. 'What's this little game?' He then admitted that he had brought it back from the beach the previous day when swimming.

I appointed one of the junior officers to take charge of the Eden island project and, on the following Sunday, we hired a motor boat and set off for the island with swimming kit and a picnic lunch. With me came the Medical and Engineer officers and a couple of NCOs from the Airfield Construction branch. The remains of the jetty looked too rotten to risk and so we anchored in a couple of feet of water and waded ashore.

The island lived up to all my expectations and my crew were delighted with what we found.

'We can do something with this,' said Bill Brown. 'There seem to be three reasonable buildings. By cutting some of these saplings, we can use them as roof timbers and stretch canvas over them. That should make the huts weatherproof for as long as we are likely to be here. I have several portable generators and electricity can easily be rigged up.'

'Now what about fresh water?' I asked; 'as this island was chosen for a lighthouse, I suspect there may be a well.'

There was, and our Medical Officer found it about a hundred yards from the huts. The well was full of rubbish but George Bowen reckoned that it could be cleaned out and the water treated if necessary. Meanwhile the Airfield Construction airmen had inspected the remains of the jetty and found that, although the planking had rotted away, the base timbers seemed sound enough and, again, we could use some of the thousands of saplings to make new decking.

We all agreed that the project was on, as we plunged into the sea to cool off before our picnic lunch and beer. The water was crystal clear with a sandy bottom and very little sharp coral. The natives at our favourite swimming village had always told us that there were no sharks and, as they all swam without fear, we felt it safe to assume they were right.

Over lunch George Bowen said that he was happy about the medical aspects provided that the well water was tested and properly treated. 'Although,' he added, 'I would advise bringing bottled water to drink, and use this well for cooking and washing. The biggest danger may be sunburn and the troops must be warned about that: reflection off this shallow water could produce severe burning even for troops as case-hardened as most of ours are.'

As we stretched out in the shade of the coconut palms discussion turned on the size, composition and duration of each party. Twelve men for four days was the general opinion, each party to be in the charge of an NCO and contain a medical orderly, a cook, and a radio operator with a set to keep in touch with the Kemajoran control tower which was no more than twenty miles away in a straight line. There were many other matters of detail to be agreed but we returned to the mainland enthusiastic about the scheme which seemed to offer at least

151

some of our hard working airmen a short break to relax in the sun.

A working party went out to Eden a few days later, stayed for three days and carried out the essential repairs to the huts, the jetty and the well, and also tested the radio link with the control tower, using the call sign 'Holiday One'. Meanwhile a description of the island and its amenities – or lack of them – was published and airmen were invited to volunteer for the four day holiday, the longest serving men in Java to be given preference. As I expected, the response was considerable and a contract was drawn up with a fisherman near our bathing beach to use his motor boat at least twice a week, or more frequently in emergency. We could afford to pay generously from canteen funds so that the airmen had nothing to pay for the brief holiday.

Flying Officer Williamson, who took charge of the scheme, selected each party and took the first one across early in February with plenty of supplies, a couple of aircraft dinghies for fishing, the necessary fishing tackle, a couple of footballs and various other things to enliven the stay.

It was a great success and each party did something to improve the accommodation until we decided to increase the numbers to eighteen, which was dictated more by the capacity of our fisherman's boat than anything else. There were no accidents or serious injuries and the scheme continued until the end of out stay in Java much later in the year. The Dakota squadron entered into the spirit of the thing and dropped mail or small quantities of supplies on the island from time to time while returning from operations. I don't know exactly how many men took advantage of these breaks but it certainly ran into hundreds.

January was an extremely wet month with rain of almost monsoon intensity on most days. Airmen were splashing about in Wellington boots, and aircraft had to be taxied with great care. The tarmac outside my office was a lake for most of the month and we were thankful that we had taken the precaution to dig drainage ditches around all our tents.

Whether the heavy rain affected the anti-British ardour of the Indonesians I don't know, but it was significant that hostile activity round Batavia died down and the Thunderbolts and Mosquitos did not fire a gun in anger during the whole month. Even so there was no slackening in the amount of operational flying and Kemajoran aircraft flew 1433 sorties during January, on convoy escorts, reconnaissance and, of course, supply and evacuation of internees.

It was at about this time that our Commander-in-Chief, General Christison came to the end of his tour. He had fought through much of the Burma campaign and had been with us in the NEI since our arrival. We were very sorry to see him go and 904 Wing not only participated in his farewell parade but provided a formation of twelve Thunderbolts to fly past the saluting base in the centre of the city. Under his command, the association between the Army and RAF had been a happy and entirely satisfactory one. Fortunately his replacement was equally as experienced in the problems of Indonesia. It was General Sir Robert Mansergh who had initially gone into Soerabaya in command of 5 (Indian) Division and remained there throughout the bitter fighting in that area. The 904 Wing squadrons down there had worked very closely with him and he was warmly welcomed when he came to Kemajoran shortly after taking up the appointment of Commander-in-Chief.

By the end of January there were distinct signs of an acceleration in the programme for the repatriation of airmen, and a steady flow of 'old sweats' going home and new airmen arriving built up. The flow out tended to be faster than the in-flow and shortages in certain trades began to cause some concern. This was due to the world-wide rundown of the RAF which had to be accepted. As, however, the pace of our operations was showing some signs of slowing down, I hoped that these shortages would not assume serious proportions. It was also apparent that the new, and usually young, airmen arriving had considerably less experience and skill than those departing.

153

The heavy rains began to ease off as February approached, but not before we suffered a particularly tragic fatal accident in which the rains may have played an important part. A Thunderbolt came in to land one morning after a heavy rainstorm, flown by a Warrant Officer pilot. He touched down satisfactorily but perhaps a little far down the runway in conditions of no wind. Whether his brakes failed or whether he aquaplaned on the flooded surface we never established, but he continued to run until he went off the far end of the runway and onto the flat, marshy ground which, under dry conditions, might have pulled him up. Unhappily his wheels sunk in and the Thunderbolt was literally tripped up and flipped over onto its back, nose first. In accordance with regulations the pilot had his cockpit canopy open for landing and, as the aircraft carried on upside down, the sloping windscreen acted as a scoop, filled the cockpit with tons of mud which pinned the unfortunate pilot back in his seat. Although the crash party was on the scene within a minute, the Warrant Officer was dead, suffocated by the mass of mud. Despite frantic efforts it took a long time to get him out, so deeply had the aircraft buried itself in the mud.

It was one of those sad accidents that one felt should have been avoided. If only the cockpit canopy had been closed the aircraft might have slid along on its roof although I think it is more likely to have been smashed with the same results. The accident served to emphasise – if any emphasis was needed – that the runway was quite inadequate for our aircraft and the loads they were required to carry.

14

Bali

The Netherlands East Indies contained a large number of islands stretching in a long string to the east of Java towards Australia. They varied greatly in size and we had been told that the majority of the smaller ones had not been regarded as sufficiently important to be occupied by the Japanese. Bali, however, was one of the larger islands and had been fortified with a garrison of about 300 Japanese troops.

According to our Intelligence sources this garrison had laid down its arms and surrendered to the local authority. The islanders were apparently in no way militant and had not taken up the surrendered weapons in the Indonesian cause. Indeed it is probable that they had little idea of what was going on in Java and Sumatra, but had simply carried on with their mainly agricultural livelihood. Communications between the outer

155

islands and Batavia were rudimentary with the result that the influence of the new Indonesian government had not so far penetrated beyond the extremities of Java. More importantly from the British point of view, there were no known internees or prisoners of war in these islands but, nevertheless, they fell within the area of the South East Asia Command and it was important to know the situation in at least the larger ones, such as Bali.

As the Indonesian government had as yet no navy and no air force, Air Commodore Stevens was asked to send a peaceful reconnaissance flight to Bali, taking a few government officials and a load of fresh meat and other supplies and to establish relations with Batavia. I was instructed to arrange the mission and take command of it myself.

The Air Commodore had on his staff an American Army Captain named Jim Morrison who was an intelligence officer. He came out to see me and announced that he had been instructed to accompany our mission as he was the nearest we had to an expert on Bali.

'You probably don't know,' he said to me, 'but I used to live in Bali before the war and built and owned a hotel by the sea close to Den Pasar, the capital. Apart from finding out about the situation in the island, I am anxious to see what happened to my hotel.'

All I knew about Bali was that it was a little known exotic tropical island, the virtues of which had been extolled in one or two films. Consequently Jim Morrison's presence was clearly going to be of immense value and I warmly welcomed it.

'Do you intend to return there after this is all over?'

'I really don't know,' he replied. 'The island has enormous potential for tourism; the people are delightful and the climate excellent, but I may have lost too much to start again if my hotel has disappeared.'

'Do you know,' I asked him, 'whether there are likely to be any supplies of aviation fuel on the island: it is almost 500 miles from here and we must be prepared to refuel, if not at Den Pasar, then at Soerabaya on the return flight?'

156

'I believe the Shell Company is operating there but I'll find out from the Shell people here for certain.'

Brian Macnamara, whom I suspected would like to do the trip himself, decided to send one of his Flight Commanders to look after me and share the flying as his squadron was exceedingly busy with a lot of maintenance problems after several months of intensive flying. As far as airfields were concerned, all we knew was that a grass or packed sand runway had existed close to Den Pasar before the war and the chances were that it was still there. It seemed reasonable to assume that the Japanese had used it.

Brian gave me one of his better Dakotas which had not carried dried fish and it was loaded with supplies provided by the government. In addition, we were to take three officials and Jim Morrison as well as two of our Air Despatch Company soldiers to supervise the unloading at the other end. One always had the anxiety that unsupervised native labour would damage the aircraft by backing trucks into it or while manhandling heavy crates. As an afterthought, we added a Sergeant Fitter, specifically to check the quality of the petrol and supervise the refuelling if suitable supplies were available in Bali.

Den Pasar was approximately 500 miles from Kemajoran and lay some distance from the eastern tip of Java. The flight should take about three and three quarter hours and, in order to ensure a full day's work there, we planned to take off at first light and reach the island by 10 am. We would remain for one night only and get back before dark on the second day. If refuelling on the return journey was necessary at Soerabaya, a second night's stay there would probably be essential, but I was anxious to avoid it.

The aircraft was loaded the night before departure and it only remained to embark passengers and crew at dawn. I agreed with Flight Lieutenant James that he would fly on the outward leg and I would fly home. He was the experienced one, the aircraft was heavily laden and we knew little or nothing about landing conditions at the other end.

The sky was just beginning to lighten as he taxied out with landing lights on. There was little wind with a clear sky which gave every promise of a fine day ahead. Dakotas never seemed to notice the load they were asked to carry and ours was no exception. She lifted off in less than 1000 yards and, as the darkness gradually faded, we climbed steadily to 8000 feet.

Three hours later we were abreast of Soerabaya when a Thunderbolt flew up alongside us. The pilot pointed to his headphones and we managed to find a common radio frequency to speak to one another. 'Good mornings' were exchanged and he reported all was well on his station. I think he was a little surprised that we weren't landing there but were going to Bali. With a final wave he half-rolled away and disappeared below us.

Forty minutes later, having left the eastern tip of Java, our island came in sight as we descended to 2000 feet to get a good look at it. Jim Morrison had come onto the flight deck and started to point out the features which he knew so well. What a peaceful sight it was; brilliant sun, blue sea and golden sand with the inevitable coconut palms and we could clearly see small figures working away in what looked like paddy fields.

'No wonder you came to live here, Jim,' I said over my shoulder as we circled with a wind sock hanging limply in one corner and a small tin roofed hut beside it.

'I would guess it to be about 1200 yards long,' chimed in James as he tightened up his turn around it, 'but there seems to be some sort of ridge running across the centre of it.'

Indeed there was a ridge which very nearly threw us back into the air again as we hit it while slowing down after a smooth and steady approach and landing.

'Just as well the Dakota was built to cope with that sort of thing,' muttered James as he turned to taxi towards the hut, which I can hardly describe as an airport terminal.

'Ah – look, aviation fuel,' I said as my eyes lighted on a familiar yellow Shell refueller standing beside the hut. Subject to its contents being checked by our Sergeant, it looked as if we would have no refuelling problems.

158

We were met by a smiling Balinese gentleman who introduced himself as the Chairman of the island's Legislative Council which I understood to be the governing body. He was extremely pleased to see us, and even more pleased to see the load of supplies in the Dakota. He led the way to an assortment of Japanese-style jeeps and small trucks, indicating that I should travel with him and the rest of the party would follow. We wound our way through the streets of Den Pasar, a delightful small town with immaculately clean streets and many Dutch colonial-type buildings. The main hotel, the name of which I can't remember, was our destination and home for the night. It was a low, rambling building with wide, open verandahs on which cold drinks were served to us by cheerful waiters clad in sarongs and the typical Javanese-style of headdress, not unlike a turban.

My first question to our host was to ask about the Japanese troops: how many, what had happened to them and where they now were. Through an interpreter, as our host's English was understandably not fluent, although he did speak it a little, he told us that there were about 300 Japanese soldiers in the police armoury and such artillery as they had was immobilised. I was pleased to hear that the Japanese had not behaved with cruelty and had left the islanders to carry on with their agricultural life. Certain beach defences had been built but, as Bali was so far from the main battle fronts and relatively unimportant, Japan had sent only second class troops who were probably only too pleased to sit back and enjoy a peaceful war in this beautiful island. There had been no information about repatriating them, which was not surprising in view of the shortage of shipping and the tens of thousands of Japanese throughout South East Asia waiting to be sent home.

It was then suggested that the government officials who had travelled with me should discuss political and administrative matters with members of the Legislative Council while the Chairman escorted Jim Morrison and me on a tour of the island.

159

'You are invited to take lunch with Monsieur Le Maire,' said the Chairman. I looked at Morrison who knew at once what this was about.

'Le Maire is a Belgian artist who has lived here since about 1932. He was one of your British Royal Academicians, and very well known, but he emigrated, and fell in love with Bali and with a Balinese dancer whom you will undoubtedly meet, and he has painted here ever since. I understand,' continued Jim, 'that he used to exhibit and sell his paintings in Singapore every few years but, when the war came, the Japanese locked him up initially, but then concluded that he posed no threat to them and so they freed him to continue with his painting which he still does in his own home. I have met him and his attractive wife whose name is Polluk.'

We set off with a driver in the best of the old jeeps, making for the beach behind which Jim had owned his hotel. Out of the town the roads were quite good and thronged with Balinese bringing vegetables and fruit into the town as it was apparently market day. All the women were bare-breasted, swinging along with baskets balanced on their heads. Most of them seemed to know our host and waved cheerfully as we passed. They certainly looked friendly and happy and one immediately had the impression that the Japanese occupation had hardly affected them. To me they were indistinguishable from the Javanese, fair skinned and attractive Polynesian people, some of the girls being very beautiful with that faintly Chinese cast of features.

As we approached Jim's beach he said, 'It's gone. You can just see where the foundations were. The Japanese have obviously demolished the hotel and cut down a lot of trees to improve the field of fire for their coastal defences, as this is probably the best beach on the island for landing.'

'I am sorry, Jim,' I said.

'Ah well, c'est la guerre,' he replied philosophically, but was clearly upset by what we had found.

'Was it insured, Jim?'

160

'It was, but not against an act of war. My wife will be upset as it was really her baby and I know she would like to come back. Can you blame her!' he said, with a wave of his arms to encompass the lush vegetation leading down to a silvery beach and deep blue sea. Our host, who clearly remembered the hotel, was very sympathetic and indicated that his people would undoubtedly help Jim to rebuild in due course.

We moved on through fields and villages until we came to one larger than the rest where our host told the driver to stop. Speaking mostly in Malay, which Jim understood and interpreted, he explained that this village wished to perform the 'Monkey Dance' in our honour that evening. He then showed us the 'theatre' where the dance would take place. It was a large circular amphitheatre, some thirty yards across, surrounded by banking on which there were wooden benches. The banks were grassy but the floor was hard-packed earth which had obviously been trodden by hundreds of dancing feet over the years.

The 'Monkey Dance', we were told was performed by 300 young men in the light of torches set high on poles around the circumference. It had not been performed during the Japanese occupation and to-night would be in honour of our arrival as representatives of the forces which had brought the occupation to an end.

The headman of the village came forward and was introduced. He was elderly and toothless but had an undoubted dignity and made us most welcome. He told us, through Jim, that his young men had been practising quietly and hoped that this first post-war performance would be a great success. We thanked him, saying how much we appreciated the honour and looked forward to something which none of us had ever seen. Even Jim Morrison, in spite of his time in Bali, had never seen the dance but had often heard about it.

'Jim,' I said, as we climbed into our jeep and left with cheerful waving and bowing, 'if I didn't have an air force career in front of me and a family at home I think I would join you here. What a delightful place.'

It was approaching lunchtime as we made our way towards Le Maire's house, also situated behind a beach flanked by coconut palms. It was a large white bungalow with the usual wide verandahs to catch every breath of breeze, for which I was extremely thankful as the brilliant midday sun had sent the temperature soaring. Bali, it must be remembered, is no more than a few hundred miles south of the Equator. I guessed the temperature was somewhere in the 90s.

Monsieur Le Maire came out to greet us: an elderly man who must have been about seventy years old, but bronzed and fit, smartly dressed in a white suit with a panama hat. He welcomed us most cordially, taking us through the house towards the rear verandah which faced the sea. I could not help noticing that every wall was hung with paintings so that hardly a square inch remained empty.

'Come and meet my wife, Polluk, and have a cool drink after your tiring morning in this heat.'

Polluk came to meet us – a beautiful, slender woman of about thirty who was a little taller than the average Polynesian woman. You could almost tell she was a dancer by the graceful way she moved, but I was surprised when she welcomed us in good English, a language which, not surprisingly, her husband spoke fluently.

We sat down in long cane chairs and were given cool coconut-flavoured drinks by a young topless girl. I commented on the number of paintings on the walls. Le Maire smiled and said, 'I have not been able to go to Singapore to sell any since 1940 and there is not much market for them here. We have survived and that is the important thing. Our needs are simple; the people are very kind and helpful to us and Polluk teaches Balinese dancing in several schools.' He talked about his initial internment, and release after a month, when the Japanese realised that he was not a spy but, as he put it, 'a harmless old artist.'

I asked if there was anything we could do for him and Polluk when we returned to Batavia. He thought for a moment or two.

162

'No, I think not, unless you can arrange for a ship to take me to Singapore to sell a hundred paintings. We had about two ships a month before the war but there has been nothing but small coastal craft and fishing boats for more than three years.'

'Can I take a few paintings back and see if KLM will fly them to your agent as their weekly aircraft passes through Singapore?' I said.

'Thank you, but I have no agent any longer and I would have to go and arrange an exhibition myself. No, I must wait until things return to normal but Polluk and I are quite happy and I still have some income.'

Lunch was served on the verandah overlooking the garden with the beach beyond. Tropical fruits seemed to abound and I could see bananas and mangoes as well as the ubiquitous coconut. The menu was soup, a local fish dish and selection of fruits. It was served by two young girls and it was a little disconcerting to find a plate of cold soup coming over one's shoulder, followed by a brown bosom. However, it is surprising how soon one can get used to anything.

As the end of a delicious lunch approached, Le Maire said that his wife would like to dance for us. 'She has her own band which she uses for teaching,' he added.

We sat back with some excellent coffee, which was apparently grown in the island, and watched a brightly coloured band of six Balinese walk onto the lawn below and settle down in one corner. Javanese music is hard to describe. Not unlike West Indian steel bands in some respects but with less rhythm and some stringed instruments as well as drums. It has a haunting quality.

Polluk, who had slipped away to change, glided onto the lawn with bells jingling at wrists and ankles, barefoot and dressed in a brilliantly coloured long skirt and brassiere. She danced for about twenty minutes with graceful movements of her head and hands. Like her music, difficult to describe unless one had seen it but most attractive. Le Maire explained the meaning of some of the movements and was clearly very proud

163

of his wife's accomplishment. Loud applause brought an end to
what had been for us a delightful interlude and we said goodbye
after another walk around some of the paintings, of which there
must have been several hundred, all of typical Balinese scenes
and people. Years later, the American magazine *Picture Post*
published a long, illustrated article on Le Maire which I
happened by chance to see and it brought back vivid memories
of this visit paid under such strange circumstances.

During the drive back to the hotel our host told us that the
Monkey Dance had been arranged for 7 o'clock and he would
take us in the jeep at 6.30 pm. The show would last for an hour
and we would dine in the hotel afterwards. This gave time for a
welcome shower and a siesta under the fan. It was extremely hot
by this time and all the workers had disappeared from the fields:
some could be seen asleep under the palm trees.

At 6.30 pm, bathed and changed into clean uniform, we set
out once more as the sun sank over the horizon with a half moon
beginning to appear. It was cooler and there was even a little
breeze off the sea, which was more than welcome as it had been
a long day since leaving Kemajoran and I was feeling quite
weary.

The village amphitheatre was now packed with people on the
benches or sitting on the grass, except for a few benches of
honour reserved for us, with the headman awaiting our arrival
and keeping villagers off our seats. We sat down after exch-
anging greetings and waving to the crowds who were outlined
against the flares now burning merrily on poles all round the
circumference. Even in the half light the flamboyant colours of
the audience made an exotic picture, and I wondered whether
Le Maire had ever painted the scene.

The band, which was much bigger than Polluk's, struck up
to loud cheering as the first of 300 young men entered the arena.
They were naked except for a loin cloth which had a monkey's
tail attached to the back of it. As soon as the dancing started, two
of the usual young Balinese beauties came along and offered
each of us half a coconut shell filled with a pale liquid. 'Coconut

milk,' I thought. Not a bit of it. James beside me took an unwise swig at it and burst into a fit of coughing. As he recovered, he murmured to me, 'God, it's lethal!' He was right. I sipped mine cautiously and, even so, felt the top of my head lift a little. It was obviously the local brew of arak.

'You find it good?' said our host with an understanding smile as he swigged half of his without the slightest effect on him.

'Excellent,' replied James with his eyes still watering. From that moment on I took very small sips and managed to tip most of it onto the grass below my seat before the attentive young ladies appeared again with a refill. I had become accustomed to Bols gin, but I knew I would never get used to arak.

While this alcoholic experience was being played out, the dancing was getting more and more frenzied as all 300 young men eventually got into the act. It didn't bear much relation to Polluk's graceful performance but it was certainly energetic and exciting. Our host made some attempts to explain the meaning of the various dances as the men switched from one routine to another but I could neither hear nor understand most of what was said.

It came to an end after an hour with a tremendous finale when all the audience cheered and stamped to the last excesses of the dancers and the band. It was fortunate that none of us were smoking, as a match dropped on all the arak under our seats would have been more than a little interesting!

For us the finale was still to come. As the headman, now full of arak and sweating profusely, ushered us back to the jeep we found it completely loaded with fruit of all kinds, a parting gift from these delightful people. It was very touching as we thanked them to the best of our ability, managed to get in the jeep and drove off into the night.

At dinner later I asked our host if there was any way we could thank his people for their kindness and hospitality.

'Don't worry,' he said with a smile, 'your visit here has convinced all my people that the years of occupation are really over, and that is more thanks than enough. We have heard stories of what is going on across the water in Java and have worried, but you and the officials you brought with you from the new government have set our minds at rest.'

After dinner James said: 'Let's have a swim from that beautiful beach outside before a nightcap and bed.'

What a good idea that was. We walked down to the sands, took off all our clothes and ran into the sea. It was glorious with the half moon now shining brightly and gentle rollers washing onto the beach. All the tiredness of a long and very hot day ebbed away. We had no towels but that didn't matter; we lay on the sand and dried off in the moonlight.

'It's a very good thing,' said James, 'that this place is too far from Batavia to use as a leave for the troops. We would never see them again.'

A final drink on the hotel verandah – no arak this time – and then to bed after deciding that there was no urgency to take off early next morning and we could give plenty of time for our civilian passengers to finish their business with the Legislative Council.

I slept like a log that night and met my colleagues for breakfast at the very reasonable hour of 8 o'clock when our civilians said they had finished their business and were very happy with the relations they felt they had cemented with the Batavian government. I was thankful that, with all the problems our forces had in Java, there was no need to be concerned about the situation in Bali and I could report accordingly to General Mansergh.

Our attentive host appeared once more to lead the convoy of jeeps back to the airstrip for a 10 o'clock take-off. The Sergeant met us and confirmed that the Shell petrol was perfectly satisfactory. The Dakota had been refuelled and he had checked over the engines. A small crowd of locals had gathered, chattering away in the background and controlled by a single policeman while we all said goodbye and James and I carried out the usual external checks on the Dakota before climbing aboard.

166

The engines started immediately and I taxied out, taking care not to cover the spectators with dust. There was a little more wind than on the previous day and as I turned at the end of the runway, James said: 'That ridge seems to me to be about 700 yards from this point. As we have very little load, you might just get off before hitting it if you hold her on the brakes for as long as possible.'

I nodded, checked that the runway was clear of animals or other obstructions and opened up the engines, releasing the brakes only when she began to move. We were very nearly airborne before hitting the ridge but a slight thump was felt as we took off. I climbed to 1000 feet and then turned to fly low down the runway again past the waving knot of spectators and climbed away into a perfect morning sky to 8000 feet.

The flight was uneventful in perfect weather. I called the tower at Soerabaya as we passed some distance from the airfield, giving my position and destination. No Thunderbolt came up to investigate on this occasion and I set course for Semarang and the coast to avoid the mountainous and volcanic centre of the island. As no lunch was likely to be forthcoming, James went back into the cabin and raided our stock of fruit. All the passengers had a lunch mainly of bananas, and very good they were. Semarang passed where one Dakota was visible on the tarmac, after which I more or less followed the coast until Kemajoran came on the air and I landed after exactly four hours. It had been my longest flight at the controls of a Dakota and a most enjoyable one. What a relief it was to have no rain and heavy clouds which had been our constant companion for about two months.

When the gift of fruit was unpacked, it was found to contain six of these dreaded coconuts filled with arak. They were complete nuts with a hole bored in the end, filled and sealed with a wooden bung. I took them along to the Mess and decided that my staff could try out this lethal drink a few nights later. What I did not know was that arak continued to ferment and should be drunk when relatively new. All the officers tried it but

167

I don't think many had more than two small glasses. Even so, the effect was, to put it mildly, considerable and we quickly decided it was not something to be indulged in.

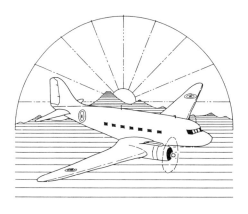

15

Offensive Operations Resumed

The month of March was much less wet than the previous two months and it was a great relief to find the lakes and puddles on the airfield beginning to dry out. But the drier weather brought its problems. The rebels, who had been so quiet since Christmas, resumed their harassing attacks and ambushes. The Thunderbolts, although they had flown as intensively as bad weather and airfield conditions would permit during January and February, had not had to open fire and had suffered no casualties.

The rebels resumed their activity and concentrated on the land links between Batavia and Bandoeng. As these were the most important cities in Java – virtually twin capitals – it was regarded as essential to maintain communications between them. The rebels clearly knew this and put their efforts into disrupting them.

As we discovered shortly after our arrival, the railway line was far too dangerous to use. It was relatively easy to sabotage tracks and bridges and create ambushes in the many wooded and hilly areas through which the railway passed. There were two road links, a southern route which was the longer but better surfaced, while a northern one, although shorter, was not at all suitable for the heavier vehicles.

The daily airlift by the Dakotas to Bandoeng continued and, if pressed, it might have been possible to keep that city supplied entirely by air but that would have meant capitulating to the rebels in endeavouring to maintain the land link, which was quite unacceptable. We did not, however, bring the internees out of Bandoeng by the road convoys. They were all flown out to avoid additional danger and suffering.

Early in March the Kemajoran Thunderbolts were called upon to cover the army during the clearance of the town of Lembang which had become a rebel stronghold from where attacks were mounted against the road convoys. Casualties were inflicted with rocket and machine gun attacks, allowing men of 23 Division to occupy the town and drive out the rebels.

This successful operation did not, unfortunately, stop the convoy attacks. During the remainder of the month the Thunderbolts were called upon to attack targets near the convoys on six occasions. Our system was, in addition to keeping at least one aircraft constantly over a convoy, to maintain Thunderbolts at immediate readiness on the airfield, fully loaded with rockets and ammunition. Every convoy had a 904 Wing Air Contact Team (ACT) with it and the officer in charge could call for support from his jeep, knowing that aircraft would be with him within ten to fifteen minutes and ready to attack any target he indicated. This scheme worked extremely well and saved many valuable Thunderbolt flying hours.

Even so, the convoys frequently had a rough passage with snipers firing from positions which were often difficult to identify. One particularly serious incident occurred 11 March near the town of Soekaboemi. A carefully planned ambush caught a large convoy close to the town and inflicted over one hundred casualties on the troops who were accompanying it to clear the area of the town. The convoy eventually fought its way through to Bandoeng but not before Thunderbolts had attacked many targets as directed by the ACT whose radio operator was wounded during the battle. These ACTs, usually comprising a Flight Lieutenant and an airman radio operator, were a constant worry to me. They were always in the thick of any incident, unprotected in their jeeps and frequently exposed while searching for a target, and then having to direct an air-craft accurately onto it. They showed immense courage and dedication to a dangerous job, often having to bring aircraft down to attack a target as close as 50 feet from the convoy vehicles. This kind of co-operation also spoke volumes for the accuracy and steadiness of the Thunderbolt pilots. On one occasion when an attack had been directed onto a large clump of bushes bordering the road, the army subsequently found ten dead Indonesians 'suitably dressed in black', indicating that they were members of the infamous 'Black Buffaloes' which had caused us so much trouble.

After this incident and other attacks in the Soekaboemi area, it was decided to switch the convoys to the northern road for both outward and return journeys. It was considered that the disadvantages of a rougher and more difficult road were more than offset by the shorter distance and the more open country with less likelihood of being ambushed. This route created problems for the Thunderbolt pilots as low cloud cover which formed in the middle of each day often made it very difficult for pilots to see the convoys and for ACTs to direct them onto their targets. Nevertheless, the most important result was that casualties were reduced and, as the days passed, the convoys met less and less hostile resistance.

By this time, 23 Division, under the command of Major General Douglas Hawthorne, had gained firm control of the area around Bandoeng and the prison camps in the neigh-bourhood were being emptied rapidly, several Dakota-loads arriving in Batavia every day. I flew up to Bandoeng in my Thunderbolt at least once a week and spent an hour or so with the Movements staff who, by now, were handling the passengers quickly and efficiently. We had found it important to give the passengers a superficial medical check before they flew because, although the flight was short – less than an hour on most occasions – many of them were so frail and ill that there was some doubt as to whether they could stand even that short flight. We did have one or two, happily very few, who died on the way down to freedom, which was tragic. When necessary an Army or RAF doctor would always accompany seriously sick passengers on these flights and the pilots had strict instructions to make the journey as smooth as conditions would allow – not always easy with the build up of cloud and rain in the middle of the day.

We lost one Dakota with its crew during a return flight from Bandoeng. What happened remained a mystery as it crashed in a dense forest some way off the direct route from Bandoeng to Kemajoran in an area which was quite unapproachable on the ground. Fortuitously the aircraft was carrying no passengers and no 'Mayday' or other distress signal was received from it. The wreckage, which appeared to be burned out, was eventually found by a Thunderbolt pilot, but it was quite impossible and much too dangerous to reach it. Whether it was shot down – which seemed unlikely – or had a catastrophic technical failure, or was struck by lightning, remained forever a mystery and once again 904 Wing mourned a casualty of this unsatisfactory campaign.

Hostile activity in the two other bridgeheads based on Semarang and Soerabaya had died down but it was still impossible for our forces to advance into the interior beyond the perimeters they had established and held strongly. Everything now depended upon the success of political negotiations and the exercise of control over the rebels by the government. Progress, albeit very slow, was however being made. A new Prime Minister, Dr Sjahrir, had acceded to the office and he was undoubtedly a man who was not only determined to gain control of the rebel factions and ensure that the remaining internees could be released from the camps in the interior, but was also prepared to reach an accommodation with the Dutch government. Many business concerns and plantations had belonged to colonial Dutch settlers before the occupation and their presence was now needed to stabilise the faltering economy of the East Indies, always provided that there was no resurgence of colonial rule. By the end of March we felt that the next few months must see a breakthrough in RAPWI's efforts to penetrate to the innermost prison camps. For the moment, however, fighting continued, particularly around the road convoys, every one of which had to be supported by the Thunderbolts with strike aircraft held at immediate readiness on the airfield.

This was the moment at which we encountered serious trouble with the Mosquitos of Wing Commander Constable-Maxwell's squadron. As many will know, the Mosquito was basically a wooden aircraft, a brilliant design evolved during the War when metal was scarce. Its performance in the European theatre had been legendary but it was not suitable for long exposure to tropical conditions.

After the war, when the supply of American Lend Lease aircraft and spares began to dry up, Mosquitos were used to maintain squadrons in both the Middle and Far East. In the Middle East, and notably in Iraq, the hot, dry climate caused the wooden and plywood construction to shrink, whereas the hot, humid conditions in South East Asia produced serious problems with the glued joints. A lack of hangar space at Kemajoran for these aircraft meant they had to remain in the open in torrential rain, intense heat and high humidity.

The result was that this splendid aircraft failed, and more and more time was involved in keeping 84 Squadron serviceable. So serious did this become that drastic action had to be taken. The same problem had arisen in Singapore and various Engineer staff officers came to discuss it at Kemajoran and inspect the aircraft.

In addition to the bomber and rocket firing Mosquito in 904 Wing, there was a Photographic Reconnaissance version, known as the PR34. This was particularly valuable, with a complex installation of cameras and also with a long range and high altitude capability. After a few more weeks and more failures, it was clearly impossible to keep our Mosquitos operating. There was an increasing risk that one would fail in the air and probably kill the crew.

In fact, Hughie Edwards had a narrow escape when he borrowed one of the bomber Mosquitos to fly up to Kuala Lumpur in Malaya. Shortly after take off on his return flight, one engine caught fire and could not be extinguished. He was close enough to Kuala Lumpur to get back and land on the airfield but, as he was actually coming to a halt on the runway, one wing burnt through and fell off. He was extremely fortunate and a less competent and experienced pilot might well have met with disaster.

The PR34 aircraft were in the middle of an important task, surveying all the areas of South East Asia before the British forces withdrew. This was an essential job for the future as many of the available maps were long out of date. Some areas had never been properly mapped.

The outcome of the technical deliberations was that only the PR34s were to be retained: all other Mosquitos were to be scrapped after salvaging engines and equipment which could be used to keep the PR34s flying for as long as possible. It was a severe blow to Michael Constable-Maxwell as we stripped and burned a large number of his aircraft. Happily it was not the end of 84 Squadron which was re-equipped in Singapore and served there for several more years. The effect of this policy was to keep the valuable PR34s flying until the last one in the RAF left the Far East on 15 December, 1955, almost ten years later.

It was a sad sight to see Mosquito fuselages burning on the far side of the airfield and being used to give practice to my Fire section in fighting aircraft fires, but nothing could detract from the achievements of this fine aircraft, mainly in the European theatre during World War II.

For some time, a visit to Java by our Supreme Allied Commander, Lord Louis Mountbatten, had been expected. The large expansion in the area of his South East Asia Command just before the Japanese capitulation in August, 1945, had created some enormous and unexpected problems, and doubtless caused him many worries. As if these problems were not enough, the continuation of active operations in the East Indies had been totally unexpected and was locking up thousands of his forces which should, of right, be enjoying the fruits of victory. He was coming to Java, as I understood, not only to visit the British forces but also to add his weight to the political pressure on the Indonesian government to liberate the many prisoners of war and internees who, eight months after the end of the war, were still languishing in camps which we could not reach.

It was 25 April when Lord Mountbatten arrived, landing at Kemajoran at 12.45 pm in his Dakota named 'Hapgift'. He was met by all the top brass in Batavia and the RAF Regiment provided a smart Guard of Honour in jungle green with pipe-clayed belts and anklets. It was very difficult for any airman to remain smart in the conditions in which we lived but I thought the Regiment did extremely well. I think that the Army would have liked the Seaforths, with their band, to provide the guard, but I was adamant. It has always been the privilege of the RAF to provide one when an important personage arrives at an RAF airfield. After a few words, the Supremo was whisked away to start his political discussions, having told us that he would like to visit the station on the following day.

Although, I was never keen for visiting senior officers to address the airmen en masse in the hot sun, this clearly had to be an exception. Mountbatten was well known for his desire to talk to troops on all possible occasions and very good at it he was.

He arrived sharp at 8 o'clock on the following morning and I had the majority of the men on parade with a suitable dais in front of them and the hangars in the background on which, I was pleased to see, were no chalked slogans about 'bloody boats.' We had passed that stage of dissatisfaction.

175

Well, his speech, which lasted for 20 minutes, was quite excellent. He bitterly regretted the position in which we found ourselves and the casualties we had suffered. He kept in daily touch with our operations and thanked the aircrews and airmen for the job being done. He told us that his talks with the Prime Minister, Dr Sjahrir, had gone well on the previous day and he expected a stronger line to be taken against the rebels, particularly those involved in attacks on the road convoys.

'You have rescued at least two thirds of the prisoners of war and internees,' he said, 'and I feel that the negotiations to allow you to fly out those still in the interior will be successful at any moment now. When that has been achieved, your work will be done and our forces should be able to leave Java during the next six months.'

This was indeed heartening news and I could see that all the officers and men of the Wing appreciated it and, what was more important, believed it. With a few final words to me he left for more visits to Army units and, I heard later, he dropped in to the Harmony Club, which was the new name given to the club set up for soldiers and airmen after the arrival on the island of the NAAFI.

Later that morning I learned from Hughie Edwards that Mountbatten would be flying up to Bandoeng at 8 o'clock on the following morning, and subsequently going on to Sumatra.

'Would you be happy, Hughie,' I said, 'if I gave him an escort of a pair of Thunderbolts as far as Bandoeng? There is a lot of hostile activity, as you well know, between here and Bandoeng, and I would be easier in my mind if we kept an eye on him in case of any incident – not that I think one is likely – and I will brief his crew to fly above 2000 feet.'

'A good idea, David, and I'm sure the Air Commodore would fully approve.'

Promptly at 7.30 pm the following morning the Supremo drove up and I took him out to his aircraft which we had moved to a position in front of the flagstaff.

'I wish my aircraft looked as smart as that,' I said, eyeing the gleaming Dakota with his flag flying from the cockpit.

'Yours work a bit harder than this one,' he replied as he said goodbye and climbed aboard.

I did not mention the escort of Thunderbolts which had taken off as he arrived and were circling out of sight. I was a little afraid he might say it was quite unnecessary, which it may have been, but I didn't want any more Dakota incidents in my parish. He departed and 50 minutes later the control tower received a radio message from the Thunderbolt leader that the Dakota had landed at Bandoeng.

Air Commodore Stevens, who had accompanied Mountbatten to the airfield came along to my office after the Dakota had left looking, I thought, very tired.

'Thank you for providing the escort. I'm sure that a lot of people in Singapore don't realise how dangerous the situation is here, and how easy it is for convoys to be shot up and aircraft to be shot down. However,' more cheerfully, 'I really do think we are on the verge of a political breakthrough. Dr Sjahrir has now reached the point of talking to the Dutch about a carefully controlled return to Java and Sumatra, and also his emissaries are slowly gaining control over the rebels. Be ready at any moment to send Dakotas into the interior to rescue the people still imprisoned in the areas of Jogjakarta and Soerakarta.

This news, on top of Mountbatten's excellent talk, was very encouraging. Before the Air Commodore left, the leader of the Thunderbolt escort came into my office to report that Lord Louis had spoken to him over the radio and thanked him for the escort which he greatly appreciated.

16

Into the Interior

The red telephone on my desk which connected me directly with Air Headquarters rang insistently: it was Hughie Edwards at the other end.

'David, we have got the breakthrough at last. Dr Sjahrir has negotiated an agreement with the rebels to allow us to fly into the interior and bring out the prisoners and internees but' – and he paused – 'there are certain conditions which must be strictly observed or the arrangement will be cancelled immediately.'

'I see, Hughie,' I said cautiously, 'I hope the conditions are acceptable: what are they?'

'Well, we are permitted to use two aircraft a day – and two only – at the airfield close to Soerakarta, called Solo. The Indonesians for their part will bring truck loads of prisoners to the airfield daily in whatever numbers we can handle in one day.

'Now,' he continued, 'the Air Commodore wants you to prepare a suitable Operation Order to cover all eventualities and to bring out the maximum number daily with the two Dakotas. No weapons are to be carried and no escorting aircraft are to be used. Can you do that in the next 24 hours?'

'Are you satisfied, Hughie, that this is really safe and that we are not going to be faced with the kind of incidents we've had in the past? I've lost six aircraft in the last few months and so I want to be quite sure about this agreement.'

'Nothing is certain or guaranteed in this place, as you well know,' he replied, somewhat curtly I thought, 'but we must obviously accept whatever risks there may be. We will arrange for RAPWI officials and a representative of the Government to accompany the first flights to see that the agreement is honoured.' With that Hughie rang off.

Well, it was excellent news and, on reflection, I felt that I might have been a little churlish to question it after the prolonged and difficult negotiations which had led to the agreement. Now to work out the details as quickly as possible. I sent for Wing Commander Ted Cotton and Brian Macnamara and we spent several hours preparing our plan.

We were told by RAPWI that Solo was quite a reasonable airfield with tarmac runways, roughish but acceptable for a Dakota. Flying time to Solo was estimated to be about two and a quarter hours, and the problem was how to make best use of the two aircraft we were allowed.

After a lot of discussion we adopted Brian's suggestion that each aircraft should fly the first two loads of passengers to Semarang and return to Solo for a second load, also to go to Semarang. After returning a second time to Solo, the last load of the day would come back to Kemajoran. Semarang was no more than some 40 minutes flying from Solo and, with about 30 passengers per flight, the two Dakotas should be able to evacuate approximately 180 people during each day. Additional aircraft would be positioned at Semarang to bring the passengers on to Kemajoran.

The timing was tight: each aircraft would do between six and seven hours flying, but it was feasible provided no undue delays occurred in loading and unloading. As none of these poor people had anything other than a little hand luggage, no heavy baggage or stores were involved. If any delays arose, then one of the two shuttle flights to Semarang would have to be omitted as it was essential that the aircraft came back before darkness fell.

I laid down very firmly that no aircrew were to remain at Solo overnight under any circumstances. If a Dakota became un-serviceable there, it was to be left as a hostage to fortune and recovered with technical assistance on the following day. Similarly, no refuelling was to be carried out at Solo as the quality of fuel, even supposing some existed, would be untrustworthy. In any case the Dakota had plenty of endurance to carry out the plan.

We then discussed the question of medical assistance. The passengers would probably be even more frail and sick than those already evacuated, having been considerably longer in captivity. The presence of a doctor to check them over seemed essential; stretchers and oxygen might well be needed. 904 Wing had only two medical officers, at least one of whom must always be on duty at Kemajoran. I decided to ask Hughie Edwards to see whether the Army could lend us two and also to see if we could borrow two more from Singapore. This aspect of our plan was extremely important as we had already ex-perienced one or two passengers dying on the flight out from captivity. In the event of having people who were seriously ill, we agreed that the medical officer on duty should hold them back for the last flight of the day and then accompany them direct to Batavia.

'I would like to send two airmen each day, probably an engine fitter and a rigger, to cope with any adjustments or minor repairs which might be needed,' said Brian, 'and if the first aircraft took a suitable pack of spares and tools, we could doubtless leave them there for future occasions. If they are pinched, too bad, but that's one of the hazards we must accept.'

To that little lot we added a spare wheel as the state of the Solo runway was not precisely known and the occasional puncture seemed a distinct possibility. As the Dakotas would be flying down to Solo virtually empty each morning, there was no problem about taking equipment and medical supplies, always provided that they were not brought back in the evening at the expense of additional passengers.

I emphasised that we must evacuate the maximum number of people each day, to which Brian added that it might well be possible to take more than 30 people on each flight as they would have little or no luggage and many of the passengers might be children. We had already found that we could sometimes strap two small children in with only one belt.

We all needed a 'cooler' after almost three hours of planning in the sticky heat of my office and a move was made back to the Wing Mess for cold beer. As we lay back in our long wicker chairs, I was about to say that I would like Brian to take the first flight and remain at Solo throughout the day, when he made the same proposal himself.

'RAPWI have no idea who will be in charge on the Indonesian side at Solo,' I said, 'but it's likely to be one of their senior people and we ought to send a fairly senior officer of our own as frequently as possible. I shall certainly go myself from time to time and maybe the two Group Captains at Air Headquarters would also like to do the trip.'

'How long is it likely to last?' asked Ted Cotton.

'Impossible to say,' I replied. 'Nobody knows accurately how many people there are in those interior camps, but they probably run into thousands. This will be our highest priority task and if Brian finds himself short of Dakotas, we will have to reduce our daily flights to Bandoeng, and possibly the daily schedule to Singapore which, in any case, could be taken on by one of the squadrons there.'

With that our meeting broke up with instructions to Ted Cotton, who had been taking notes throughout, to prepare an Operation Order to go to the Air Headquarters the following day. I jumped into my car and went off to see Hughie Edwards and give him the gist of what we had decided. He was very happy with it, as was the Air Commodore, and he promised to do his best to find more medical officers who, to my mind, were going to play a critical part in the operation.

Ted worked most of the night on the Operation Order and made a good job of it so that we were able to get it up to the Air Commodore by lunchtime the next day. After a short pause, I was told that the first rescue flight was to go in two days time and would be accompanied by one of Dr Sjahrir's ministers to ensure that the agreement was fully understood and that both sides abided by the rules. This news was a relief to me as I was a bit concerned about sending our aircraft deep into the interior which had been denied to us for so long.

Brian led his two Dakotas down the runway at dawn and disappeared into the clear light of what promised to be a fine day. An hour later two more aircraft set off for Semarang to pick up the first passengers who would be taken there from Solo, followed two hours later by a second pair to collect those from the next shuttle. The operation for which I had waited for more than six months had started, and I could only sit back anxiously for the results.

One of the Semarang Dakotas called the tower at 11 o'clock to alert Joan Vickers and her Red Cross team, reporting 30 passengers, two of whom were on stretchers. I drove out to meet the aircraft as it taxied slowly in to its parking bay. Even though I was accustomed to seeing emaciated and ill people disembark I was shocked by the frailty and condition of this first load of passengers from Solo. Almost without exception they had to be helped down the steps from the Dakota, most of them desperately thin with swollen bellies and legs, the sure signs of beri-beri and malnutrition. The small fleet of Red Cross ambulances took them away but not before they showed their happiness by laughing and crying and thanking Flight Lieutenant James, who had flown them in. He came over to Joan Vickers and myself and said:

'The second Dakota is about an hour behind us and, as far as I can tell, everything is going smoothly at Solo. We passed the second pair of aircraft going into Semarang as we left.'

My own doctor was on the spot and both he and Joan Vickers were perturbed at the condition of some of the passengers. She hurried away to make more arrangements for their care, saying, 'If we are going to have 180 a day as frail and ill as this, we are going to have medical problems. What we need is a couple of large hospital ships, but there's no hope of that. Never mind, we'll cope somehow.'

The last Dakota, flown by Brian Macnamara, landed in the twilight, carrying eight stretcher cases and the doctor, making our total for that first day 160 evacuees. After seeing his patients into the hands of the Red Cross, the doctor and Brian came over to my office and slumped gratefully into chairs with a whisky and soda each.

'Well, what's the verdict?' I asked. The doctor said he was very concerned at the condition of some of the passengers.

'One thing we must do is to take suitable food and drink to Solo each day. There is nothing for them to eat or drink there, and heaven knows what they had, if anything, before leaving the camps at dawn.'

'What is the attitude of the Indonesians?' I asked.

Brian spoke up and said the day's work had gone satisfactorily but there was no doubt that the Indonesians were sullen and pretty uncooperative. He said that the airfield at Solo was adequate – just – but it was surrounded by guards lying in the long grass with rifles and machines guns.

'The minister and RAPWI representatives who came with me were very helpful but I gained the firm impression that any unfortunate incident could spell disaster for the agreement. 'However,' he continued, 'we must get these poor people out and be patient over any delays or problems which arise, and there probably will be some.'

The provision of food and drink created a new problem.

'Drink is more important than food which, in any case, must

be light and digestible. The temperature at Solo is in the 90s at midday and there is very little shade or shelter,' said the doctor.

It began to look as if we were over-stretching ourselves in planning to deal with 180 evacuees a day but it was vital that none of them had to be sent back to a prison camp at night. I reported this to Air Headquarters and asked Sorel-Cameron if he would try to get the Red Cross, perhaps with help from the Army, to provide a daily pack-up of suitable food while I would cope with the drink in thermos containers. We also agreed to reduce our daily commitment to 150 people which would provide a small cushion against unforeseen problems such as bad weather and aircraft unserviceability. It would also relieve the Red Cross of 30 casualties a day.

Before Brian left my office he said, with a grin, 'I'm sure you would like to know who is in charge at Solo. It's none other than your old friend General Subidio, who crashed his aircraft here a few months ago.' I wasn't quite sure whether that was good or bad news, but I was to find out in due course.

During the next few days the weather remained fine and the evacuation continued satisfactorily with approximately 150 coming in each day. Joan Vickers and her hard worked helpers were managing splendidly, aided by the arrival of a large passenger liner from Holland. It became noticeable that the number of stretcher cases and seriously ill people declined which indicated that the Indonesians were getting rid of these categories first. There was also a high proportion of women and children in the early consignments which made me think that men, particularly those of military age, were being held back, doubtless as hostages should the agreement collapse. By the end of the first week we had evacuated almost 1000 without any serious incidents and only one puncture and a couple of radio failures which created a temporary emergency until the Dakota concerned appeared out of the gloom one evening without warning and received an immediate green light from the control tower.

It was time for me to look at the conditions at Solo for myself and see whether there were any improvements we could make

184

for the comfort of our passengers. Accordingly I took the first Dakota flight on the 21 May. Brian treated me to a refurbished aircraft newly arrived from a major overhaul at Singapore. I took off at dawn and, with Flight Lieutenant Jackson as my co-pilot, climbed away into a clear sky. On this occasion we had one of the RAPWI staff officers, my own senior medical officer and two airmen on board with a good supply of drinks and food.

Our course lay over the mountainous and volcanic backbone of the island which I had only seen previously from a distance. Looking down from 10,000 feet, it was easy to see that it was perfect guerrilla country. Our relatively small British forces could not possibly have penetrated it from their restricted bridgeheads against the type of opposition which we had already met elsewhere.

As the mountains gave way to a flat, heavily cultivated plain, I came down to 2000 feet and Jackson, who had been there on an earlier flight, pointed out Soerakarta in the distance and the position of the airfield.

'There is no radio,' he said, 'and you won't get any green light or assistance in landing. It is simply a matter of flying round, checking that the runway is clear and going in.'

Well the runway looked all right, about 1600 yards I guessed, but the thing that struck me was that the grass was at least three feet high, more like a field of hay than the borders of an airfield, and I could distinctly see the guards lying in the grass with their weapons at the ready. I made a careful approach and a reasonable landing on a tarmac surface which was as rough as Kemajoran had been when we had arrived. We jolted to a standstill and turned off towards a collection of huts, came to a halt and switched off.

I was not prepared for what happened next as I put on my battered gold braided hat and climbed out. Sure enough, the small General, whom I at once recognised as Subidio, came marching out to meet me without a smile or any sign of welcome on his face. Before I could even say 'Good morning, General,' he loosed off a string of Malay, of which I didn't understand a word, but which sounded threatening.

While I was looking round for some help to interpret this tirade, as that is what it seemed to be, a white woman of about forty with flaming red hair came up behind the General, saying, 'Can I help?' She had a strong Australian accent and I afterwards learned that this was the famous 'Soerabaya Sue' who had broadcast for the Japanese during the war and then for the Indonesians.

'The General wants to know why you are flying a Dutch aeroplane?'

This rocked me back on my heels. I said I was sorry but I didn't understand: the General had been to Kemajoran and knew that I was the Commanding Officer there. 'Why,' I asked, 'should I want to fly a Dutch aircraft?'

As she translated this to Subidio, I noticed that he kept pointing to something over my shoulder. I turned and realised it was the red, white and blue RAF roundel on the Dakota fuselage which was exciting him. I very nearly burst out laughing but caught myself in time to avoid what looked like developing into a delicate situation. I explained to our interpreter that these were the normal peacetime RAF insignia and, although the Dutch used the same colours, their configuration was different.

Of course it would happen at that moment that the second Dakota taxied in and Subidio at once pointed to its blue and white roundels with the red omitted. At some length I explained that, during the War, all Dakotas in Burma had the red in their roundels painted out to avoid confusion with the 'rising sun' emblem of the Japanese who had a transport aircraft very like the Dakota. A long, and to me quite unintelligible, harangue then took place between Sue and Subidio while I waited somewhat impatiently to hear the outcome.

'The General knows very well who you are,' she said, 'but your aeroplane is different to others and, although he believes your explanation, you were very lucky not to have been shot down by his guards when coming in to land. He says you are not to use this aeroplane to-day, and you must take it back to Kemajoran empty.'

Curbing my impatience with difficulty, I again explained the difference between the markings on the two Dakotas, but it was to no avail – Subidio was adamant. Finally I said to Sue, 'Tell the General that I must accept his decision.'

With that I turned on my heel and walked away before I said something which might endanger the whole operation. As I walked towards the first load of passengers who were being documented and medically checked, Flight Lieutenant Jackson, who had overheard the whole incident and who could see I was furious, caught up with me.

'Sir, may I make a suggestion?'

'Anything, Jackson, if it will help to solve this cock up.'

'I think,' he continued, 'that if we get cracking we could do three trips to Semarang with the one aircraft. When Wilson returns from the second one, I would take over, do the third and arrive back at Kemajoran just after dark.'

As I looked a little doubtful, he went on, 'I am more experienced than Wilson and have done a lot of night flying on Dakotas. Also the weather looks stable. Wilson could go back with you as co-pilot and you could arrange for a flare path to be laid out for me. I know the approaches well enough not to be worried about the lack of obstruction lights.'

Jackson's proposal would result in 120 passengers being evacuated that day and so, after a little more discussion, I agreed to it; it was a very sensible solution which, in my fury, I certainly had not come round to thinking of.

I called Flight Lieutenant Wilson over and told him about the new plan. He agreed wholeheartedly and promised to turn round at Semarang as quickly as possible and also to let them know there what had happened. Semarang had communications with Batavia and it should be possible to get another Dakota down to take the third load of passengers within the hours of daylight. If that were not possible, it was preferable for

187

that load to stay at Semarang for the night under British protection than to remain at Soerakarta.

'It would speed up my turn round,' said Wilson, 'if I had no stretcher cases to unload at the other end.'

Wilson did very well and landed back from his second trip by 2 o'clock with the third load all checked and ready to emplane with Jackson at the controls. I decided I must be away in my useless Dakota by 3 o'clock for the two and a half hours flight home with time to arrange for Jackson's arrival in darkness.

I spent most of the day checking the arrangements for feeding and examining the evacuees who were undoubtedly a little fitter than many of the earlier ones we had seen, but still weak and sickly. There were only four stretcher cases, none very serious and the doctor reckoned they could await the last flight to Kemajoran which we calculated should take off at about 5 o'clock.

Soerabaya Sue and I sat under a Dakota wing in the shade while I thanked her for her help. She was a strange, mixed-up lady and I couldn't understand why or how she had become the 'Lady Haw-Haw' of South East Asia. It was no business of mine however, and I was grateful to her for helping me in a difficult and sensitive situation. Subidio, meanwhile, had disappeared in his car, for which I was thankful as we had nothing more to say to one another. It was obvious that I mustn't allow another Dakota to come to Solo with red, white and blue roundels. We must stick to our blue and white markings and erase any red for as long as we remained in Java.

On reflection I decided that it was fortunate that it was I who was flying the new aircraft because, at least, Subidio knew me. Had it been one of the junior squadron officers who brought it to Solo, he could have found things very difficult as Subidio had been determined to make up for his loss of dignity at Kemajoran some months earlier. He could well have placed the whole evacuation agreement in jeopardy. I made up my mind not to make a scene about the incident in Batavia: the welfare of the evacuees was the most important aspect and we could easily repaint our aircraft where necessary and let Subidio have his little triumph. Nevertheless, the incident showed how extremely delicate and finely balanced the political agreement was.

The afternoon went smoothly and Jackson got away to Semarang on the third flight at about 2.45 pm, which meant that he should be back at Solo by about 4 o'clock. I decided that I would take all the ground staff except the doctor and one airman back with me, leaving the maximum number of seats for the evacuees on the last flight of the day, trusting to luck that nothing would go wrong with Jackson's aircraft.

I taxied out with Wilson beside me and took off through the long grass with guards still lying beside the runway with their weapons at the ready, hoping that Subidio had issued instructions that I was not to be regarded as a suitable target. All was well and we climbed away towards the mountains.

'You've had a tiring day,' I said to Wilson. 'You must have turned round quickly at Semarang.'

'It went very smoothly,' he replied 'and the Dakota crews from Kemajoran really buckled down to it when I explained what had happened. In fact I only stopped one engine – on the door side – to avoid blowing the passengers away.' I made a mental note to tell Brian Macnamara of the excellent performance of his two Flight Lieutenants.

It was a pleasant and easy trip and two hours later I called Kemajoran and received a clear reply at a distance of some 40 miles. I told them briefly that the second aircraft would be returning after dark with a full load of passengers and would need the flarepath to be laid out. We only possessed goose neck flares which were small watering cans, filled with paraffin and a wick protruding from the snout. They gave very little light for landing but they outlined the sides of the runway and were quite adequate for experienced pilots. It was also necessary for the control tower to warn the Red Cross to arrange for the reception of the late arrivals who would include some stretcher cases but, I understood, no very serious cases.

My instructions were acknowledged and 20 minutes later we were dropping down over Tandjoeng Priok as the light began to fade, but it was a beautiful, calm evening and Jackson shouldn't have any problems. As I landed, airmen were wheeling out the trolleys of flares to be placed at intervals down the sides of the runway and at the approach end of it to indicate the threshold.

It had been a long, hot and tiring day and a large, cold beer was an urgent necessity. Brian met me as I climbed out with just such a beer in his hand; it reinforced my intention to put him up for a DSO in due course.

'What's been going on? I've had all kinds of garbled reports including one that you had a punch up with an Indonesian General.'

After a long pull at my beer, we climbed up the wooden ladder to the control tower and I gave Brian an account of what had happened. I think he wanted to roar with laughter but could see that I was very tired and still furious.

'There are two things we must do at once, Brian. Firstly ensure that the red in any of our Dakota roundels is painted out and secondly, that a reasonably senior officer goes to Solo every day. Although we got through today, I wouldn't put it past Subidio to find some excuse to delay our operations. It's bad enough seeing these evacuees when they arrive here but I thought they looked even worse when they reached Solo from the camps in a series of ancient three-ton trucks. Nothing must stop us from finishing off this job even if we have to put up with a few irritating objections and delays.

'I quite agree,' he replied, 'I'll go there myself tomorrow.'

We remained in the tower and shortly after 7 o'clock Jackson came on the air, saying that he was 30 miles away and had 32 evacuees on board, of whom four were on stretchers. The flares were lit and very soon his navigation lights came into view. He carried out a wide descending sweep of the airfield over the city and came in for a perfect landing on the flarepath. With floodlights illuminating the parking area, the reception party was ready and soon had all the passengers offloaded and on their way to what I hoped was the happiest and most comfortable night they had had in years. Jackson came up to the tower and I thanked him for a really excellent day's work. His only regret was having to leave 23 possible passengers behind at Solo.

'But I promised them that they should have priority to-morrow,' he said as he too sank a long, cold beer.

After a quick count of passengers, we found that 128 had been brought out during the day which was a good effort for what amounted to the work of a single Dakota.

On the following morning I drove up to Air Headquarters and reported the previous day's incident. The Air Commodore took me to see General Mansergh who was a little perturbed about the stability of the agreement but when I said that I thought Subidio was trying to exert his authority which had been damaged by his undignified accident at Kemajoran, it was decided not to mention it to Dr Sjahrir and his officials.

No further difficulties were experienced at Solo and the evacuation continued every day for two more months with only the occasional hiccup due to some minor problem with an aircraft. What surprised me was the impressive way in which the Red Cross and the RAPWI organisations managed to handle not only as many as 150 evacuees from Solo every day but also quite a number from the Bandoeng area as well.

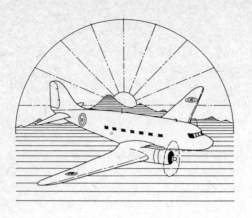

17

A Glimpse of Peace

It was a Sunday night in June as I tossed and turned on my hard camp bed in our strange little Mess, with a useless ceiling fan churning the overheated air lazily above my head. For several weeks the heat had been intense and was forecast to continue for at least the next couple of months.

I had been out to 'Eden Island' for a picnic and swimming with half a dozen of my officers, probably getting a touch of sunstroke in the process, although it had been a delightful and relaxing day. The air was no cooler out on the verandah when I got out of bed in an attempt to get a little more air. My drinking water was tepid and altogether it was a wretched night.

However, I pulled myself together by reasoning that, after eight months in Java, we must be more than half way through our stay. Our task of evacuating the internees was at last going well and there could not possibly be many more than the thousands we had already brought out to safety. It would do me good. I thought, to go down once more to Solo, partly to show General Subidio that he had not deterred me, but mainly to see if it was at all possible to get an idea of how many more people there were still to be brought out. Even at this late stage the efficient RAPWI staff had no more than a sketchy idea of what camps existed in the interior and where they were located. Interrogation of those who had already been brought out led RAPWI to believe that they had identified all the camps, but there was always that slight fear that the Indonesians were holding back internees, possibly in a camp not yet identified, to act as hostages should the agreement collapse. On balance that was not thought to be the case, but as long as active opposition continued, for example on the Batavia-Bandoeng road, that fear could not be entirely disregarded. These random thoughts were sufficient to send me to sleep on that sultry Sunday night, and I was able to start the day's work on Monday with what I often describe as 'renewed animosity.'

Two days later I flew to Solo again, this time taking a Dakota with our old blue and white markings. Little seemed to have changed: the grass was even longer and the guards were still lying in it with their weapons at the ready. I even saw one out of the corner of my eye raise his rifle and aim at me, but nothing came out of the spout.

My co-pilot, once again Flight Lieutenant Wilson, did the two flights to Semarang while I looked into affairs at Solo. Neither Subidio nor Soerabaya Sue were there on this occasion and I spent the day with the passengers while the doctor, from Singapore this time, worked away with his examinations and my Movements officer took down what particulars he could and allocated people to the aircraft. This documentation was a great help to the Red Cross at Batavia apart from providing the necessary manifest for each aircraft in case anything untoward happened to it. The whole thing was very rough and ready but the best that could be done under a canvas awning in great heat.

I quizzed a lot of the fitter passengers who were anxious to talk about their experiences while they consumed the food and drink we had brought.

'Please don't eat too much,' the doctor told them. 'You have quite a long flight in front of you and, hungry though you may be, you must take things gently for a while.'

After talking to them, I came to the conclusion that we probably had identified all the camps. This particular party came from three, and none of them had any knowledge of any camps which were not being evacuated. This was not my business, of course, and the RAPWI staff in Batavia would be interrogating many of them later, and obviously keeping a careful list of the camps from which they came. Nevertheless it cheered me to feel that the end of our task might well be in sight.

Wilson returned from his second trip to Semarang at about 2.30 pm and we loaded our passengers and I took off a few minutes after 3 o'clock with 25 internees and our own staff who had worked at Solo throughout the day. Climbing over the mountains the weather began to deteriorate, thick and ominous cloud forming ahead. As we reached it, the turbulence increased and the old Dakota started to wallow about in its customary way. I tried various heights but it was pretty rough everywhere. We left the mountains behind and dropped down to 5000 feet with no improvement. It was no great worry to me but I was concerned for the passengers.

Wilson and I discussed the problem and he suggested very sensibly that we should fly out to sea and then up the coast to Batavia at about 2000 feet. It was certainly less bumpy over the water but we then ran into heavy rain which drummed on the roof with the wipers going at full speed.

I asked for the doctor to come up to the flight deck and he reported that half a dozen of the passengers were feeling sick but there were no serious problems. An hour later the rain lessened a little and it was possible to see the coast more clearly. I wanted to keep about a mile out to sea with enough height to reach the beach if anything went wrong. Shortly after this Kemajoran

194

came within range and I was told that it was raining only slightly after a storm, and the runway was flooded but serviceable. The heavy wear and tear on our runway over the months had created indentations all over the Bit Hess, allowing large puddles to form which were always slow to drain as the runway had virtually no camber on it.

I flew a wide circuit in the mist and light rain, touching down, as usual in these conditions, like a destroyer. The Dakota came to rest with water dripping from every surface and I taxied slowly into the parking area. Even though some of the passengers had felt ill and airsick, they were so thrilled with their first flight to freedom that they soon forgot the small inconvenience.

On the following day I discussed the situation with the RAPWI staff in the city. They told me that they calculated that we should have cleared all the prisoners of war and internees from the known camps within about a fortnight, that is by early July; and furthermore, they were as certain as they could be that no more unidentified camps existed. Most of the people from camps in the Soerabaya area had been shipped out to Singapore from that port. There were no more to be rescued from the region of the Semarang bridgehead and all that now remained was to finish off the Solo operation and evacuate the last few people from Bandoeng. Once they were all concentrated in Batavia, it was a matter of awaiting suitable shipping and aircraft.

Needless to say this news was an immense relief to me. The resources of 904 Wing were being considerably stretched, partly by the repatriation of airmen according to the release programme which had at last got into top gear, partly by the inexperience of most of the replacement airmen and partly because the serviceability of Thunderbolts and Dakotas was falling due to lack of engines and spares, not to mention the heavy wear and tear of the last few months. Both of these types were American Lend Lease aircraft, supplies for which had virtually dried up since the end of the war.

195

Many changes were to take place during the next two months. To me the most surprising was an agreement between the Indonesian government and that of Holland to allow Dutch military personnel back into the East Indies. It was surprising in view of the intense hostility towards the Dutch which had been so evident since our arrival.

I learned of this agreement when Air Commodore Stevens came out on one of his occasional visits to Kemajoran and told me that the Dutch Air Force were coming back to their old station at Tjililitan which lay a short distance from the city on the opposite side to Kemajoran.

'I also believe,' he said, 'that they will be allowed to take over from you when our task is finished. They have a small twin engined bomber squadron of American B25 (Mitchell) bombers which could operate from here and help you with the convoy protection task.'

When I said how surprised I was at this development he continued; 'It has all happened rather quickly, I agree, but the Indonesian government know full well that we are not intending to remain after all the internees have been accounted for, and that should be fairly soon. Once that task is completed, we must pack up and go, and avoid getting involved in more political problems.

'Knowing that,' the Air Commodore went on, 'the Indonesians must have some military support to help them to pacify the country, and so they have invited Dutch elements to return under strict conditions.'

'Well, I would certainly welcome a few B25s to help out with the convoy protection. It is occupying many flying hours and my one Thunderbolt squadron is hard pressed to maintain the number of patrols needed. The lack of spares and the working conditions for servicing are now beginning to reduce the serviceability of the squadron.'

We agreed that I should fly up to Tjililitan to see what assistance the Dutch could offer us, and this I did a few days later with Ted Cotton in a Harvard which had been allotted to us earlier. The flight took 20 minutes and was interesting as the Dutch airfield lay to the west of the city in an area which had hitherto been a forbidden zone since our bridgehead did not extend to the west of Batavia.

We were cordially received and had a long discussion, the outcome of which was that four Mitchells of their 18 Squadron, which I understood had been in Australia for most of the war, would be based at Kemajoran under my operational control and participate in the escorting of the Bandoeng convoys. My only fear, which I did not voice at this meeting, was that the visible presence of Dutch aircraft at Kemajoran might increase hostile acts against the airfield in spite of the fact that General Mansergh's forces had cleared up most of the problems in the Batavia area.

In the event my fears were groundless and the four Mitchells duly arrived and their crews, all of whom spoke perfect English, threw themselves into the task allotted to them with great enthusiasm. It was quite clear that this step heralded the start of the reduction of 904 Wing and the first tangible glimpse of the end of its task.

By the end of June the news came through that 60 Squadron – my Thunderbolt squadron which we had originally sent to Soerabaya – was to return to Kemajoran, and that Pat Kennedy's 81 Squadron was to be disbanded. All the British forces were pulling out of Soerabaya where no more internees were left to be evacuated. At that end of the island our job had been finished and, with the Semarang bridgehead also to be evacuated shortly, the remaining British forces were concentrated in the Batavia/Bandoeng area which continued to be unsettled with the latter city still being supplied by road and air.

Although 81 Squadron was formally disbanded as a Thunderbolt squadron at the beginning of July, the name was carried on in Singapore where it was reconstituted as a Photographic Reconnaissance unit equipped with the Mosquito PR34: it continued in that guise for a further nine years.

I had a disbandment parade on the tarmac with the band of the Seaforth Highlanders borrowed for the occasion to lend tone – and plenty of colour – to the parade which finished with a fly-past of twelve Thunderbolts from the squadron. After a fine record in Burma, it had an even more meritorious performance in Java when it flew more than 2000 operational hours with countless accurate attacks on rebel strongholds. Five members of the squadron were killed in Java, two in the air and three on the ground. Their names are recorded for posterity on a memorial.

I was sorry indeed to lose Pat Kennedy who had not only been a fine squadron commander with a wealth of fighter experience, but had also been a great help to me with all the problems we had faced together. Some of his pilots joined 60 Squadron on its arrivals from Soerabaya and continued to fly Thunderbolts until the end of our stay in the island.

As the Wing began to slim down the pressure on our extremely limited accommodation eased somewhat. We kept all the houses along the one side of the street opposite the brothels and could reduce the number of airmen in each room from about five to three. Sanitation, however, continued to be a dreadful problem and no amount of pressure could persuade the municipal authorities to improve it. As for the ladies of leisure in the houses opposite, they seemed to strike up an extraordinary form of 'platonic' friendship with the troops, and my initial fears were unfounded. The airmen had undoubtedly taken our doctor's frequent warnings to heart and the girls, for their part, seemed to have accepted that there would be little or no trade from across the road and settled down to a cheerful and friendly relationship. I must admit that it astonished me but also impressed me with the sense of responsibility shown by the men.

It was a time of much greater stability in Batavia. Entertainments at the Box Club and Harmony Club were now quite frequent and sporting fixtures had begun to be arranged, a situation which would have been impossible six months earlier.

904 Wing won a football competition against the best that the Army and local civilian teams could produce. My padre had, with the help of a few dedicated airmen, created a small chapel from the derelict house at the entrance to the station. It seated about 30, and when the Bishop of Singapore arrived to hold a Confirmation Service I felt that we really were returning to a civilized way of life.

With some regret we had to discard the jungle uniform which had been such a serviceable and, I thought, smart form of dress. No more supplies existed, but in any case, all new arrivals came in khaki drill and green had long since disappeared in Singapore and elsewhere. To appear at the Command Headquarters in jungle green would undoubtedly have brought forth the accusation that you were 'shooting a line.' The RAF Regiment alone retained their green uniform with white belts and anklets. When ten years later I was in command of a large bomber station in Lincolnshire with, perhaps, 500 smartly and uniformly dressed airmen on parade, I would cast my mind back to Ulunderpet and Kemajoran and remember that motley body of men, some in khaki and some in jungle green. Motley they may have been but their conscientious efficiency and dedication to the job in hand were beyond praise.

So many rumours filled the air towards the end of July about the future of British forces in Java that I decided to fly up to Singapore myself and see what I could find out about 904 Wing's future. It was now the only one of the many mobile Wings which had formed Paddy Bandon's Group in India twelve months earlier. All the others had been disbanded in the various areas of South East Asia which they had occupied after the fall of Japan. It seemed pretty clear that the Wing could not continue for very much longer, but the many rumours needed investigating. Quite apart from that, I was anxious to know what would happen to me as I was now only half way through the normal three year tour in the Far East.

I asked Brian Macnamara if I could fly the daily scheduled service to Singapore, to which he readily agreed and I set off early in the morning of the 30th July. It was a clear, bright morning giving promise of a beautiful day as we climbed away to the north over the docks, carrying some freight and mail as well as 12 very happy airmen on their way home.

Three hours and forty minutes later we were over Singapore island. The harbour was packed with shipping and I could see two warships moving slowly up the Johore Strait towards the Naval dockyard. Kallang had, since my previous visit, become entirely a civil airport, the RAF transport force having moved to Changi, situated at Fairy Point overlooking the Strait. This was the home of the Command Headquarters, a fine modern station which had originally been built for the Army, but which was allocated to the RAF after the war, mainly because the Japanese had built an airfield there. The runway was still overlaid with PSP and it produced the well known bow wave ahead of us as I touched down with the usual tortured clatter from the PSP. How I hated that stuff, but I must admit that it had been invaluable. I suppose we had to be grateful to our erstwhile enemies for making it almost inevitable that Changi should be given to the RAF but it upset the Army very much as it was a well built and excellent station in all respects.

The Commander-in-Chief's pilot, Peter Helmore, walked out to meet me, saying that Sir George Pirie, who had succeeded Sir Keith Park, wanted to meet me, and then the Senior Air Staff Officer would discuss the future.

Changi was a most interesting station, quite unlike any other in the RAF. Built on the hilly promontory of Fairy Point which stuck out into the Johore Strait, it consisted of a series of spacious barrack blocks which had been partitioned and now served as the Command Headquarters. All the offices were approached by wide verandahs running round each block, with spectacular views over the Strait. From the headquarters the ground sloped steeply down to the airfield far below on level ground. Fairy Point Mess for senior officers stood on the topmost pinnacle, a most attractive white building which dominated everything else. Having been built pre-war to very high standards, it really was an exceptional and comfortable station. As I climbed the steep hill to the C-in-C's office, little did I know that six months later I would be Mess Secretary of the Fairy Point Mess, among other duties, of course.

Sir George Pirie was most generous in his praise of all we had done, and were still doing in Java. He was a very able and cultured man and it was no great surprise that, when he retired some time later, he studied Law and qualified as a Barrister. There can't be many of his age and rank to start such a new and challenging career.

'When you come out of Java and your Wing is disbanded,' he said, 'I want you to go home on mid-tour leave, and when you come back, to complete your tour in this Headquarters. I must tell you, however, that you will have to drop a rank, back to Wing Commander.'

Before I could recover from this shock, he continued, 'As the RAF reduces to its peacetime size, all acting ranks are being abolished and hundreds of regular officers are coming down in rank. Indeed, one or two are dropping two ranks, and so you must accept it in the right spirit. I can assure you that you'll get full credit for the work which 904 Wing is doing in Java. That won't be overlooked.'

Initially this was a bit of a facer but, when I thought about it, I realised that so many of my contemporaries were in the same position and it was quite logical.

'Well, sir,' I said, 'that solves one of my problems,' picking up my terrible Indian-made Group Captain's cap. 'I haven't been able to replace this, and now there is no need.'

'Not yet,' he replied, 'but you'll be able to save up for a new one in due course. Come along to the Mess and have some lunch.'

During the remainder of the day, I called on various members of the staff who all told me what I had expected, namely that, as soon as General Mansergh was satisfied that we had evacuated all known prisoners of war and internees, he would give the order to leave Java. 904 Wing would be disbanded and it was generally thought that the Dutch would be permitted by the Indonesian government to take over Kemajoran.

The question of my home leave was raised. Mid tour leave, usually of one month at home, was a privilege granted to all who were serving on a three year tour in the Far East. Until very recently no families had accompanied their menfolk and it was not until 1946 that married quarters and other family accommodation became available, and then not in all parts of the Command. Consequently most of the RAF took advantage of the mid tour break and were flown home by Transport Command. It was left to me to decide when the work of my Wing was virtually over and I could leave a Wing Commander to oversee the final departure.

After a convivial evening and comfortable night in the Fairy Point Mess, I was driven down to the airfield to take the Dakota schedule back to Java.

It was the 1st August and, although I did not know it at the time, it was to be my last flight in a Dakota. What a remarkable workhorse that aircraft was! Easy to fly, totally reliable and forgiving to those who, like myself, sometimes made mistakes.

The weather was perfect with a glittering sea below us and the thousand islands looking like everybody's dream of a desert island. As I approached Batavia, I dropped down to 1000 feet and decided to take a look at our 'Eden Island' holiday camp which was as popular as ever. I flew slowly round it and could see several airmen swimming and others lying naked on the sand. A thin column of blue smoke was rising from the cookhouse as lunchtime drew near.

'You are number one and clear to land' came the voice of the Controller as we neared Kemajoran, three hours and twenty minutes after leaving Changi. The station looked quiet and peaceful – and dry – so very different I thought, from the mud and rain of a few months earlier. It was almost mid-day as I landed and very hot indeed as I put on the battered cap and climbed down the steps.

202

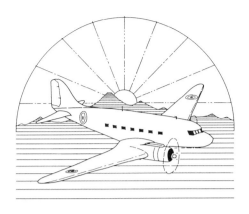

18

Last Months in Java

By the middle of August it was apparent that the Indonesian government had signed some form of comprehensive agreement with the Dutch government for the return of considerable Dutch forces to the island as, in addition to the air force squadron which had joined me at Kemajoran, Dutch navy and army personnel began to appear in the streets of Batavia.

One immediate effect of this increased Dutch presence was a violent upsurge of rebel activity, notably on the road to Bandoeng and in that town itself. We all felt that this was in the nature of a last fling against authority but, nevertheless, the Thunderbolts and Mitchells were kept busy escorting the road convoys, and it was necessary for me to maintain the standby fighters daily to go to the support of the convoys if called for by the Air Contact Teams. We had thought that the 'Black Buffaloes' and other gangs had been virtually brought under control, but here was proof that Dr Sjahrir and his Ministers had not yet obtained undisputed authority over the whole country and that hostility towards the Dutch was still present, if not as widespread as before.

By this time the majority of the remaining Japanese troops were being shipped home: their passive support of the rebellious gangs no longer existed and, furthermore, the weapons and ammunition which they had originally handed over had largely been used up. There is no doubt that, as far as we were concerned, the Japanese had managed to prolong the war for at least twelve months.

It was significant that the resumption of violence put a temporary stop to our daily Dakota flights in and out of Solo, leaving a small residue of people still to be evacuated. Fortunately this hiatus did not last long and we were able to restart the daily flights and clear the last of the prisoners from their internment during early August. This incident highlighted the extreme sensitivity of the situation and I was fearful that it might result in the infiltration of Dutch forces being slowed down and so delay the completion of our task and departure from the island.

August also saw the attachment of Dutch personnel, mainly officers, to various sections of 904 Wing to learn how to run the station in preparation for taking over. They came into the Operations and Intelligence sections, Air Traffic Control and many of the administrative sections. Understandably they had a great deal to learn and the transition was not going to be easy. For example, in no circumstances could we allow them to attack rebel hideouts on the Bandoeng road. This could only be done, if necessary, by the Thunderbolts called up from standby on the airfield. Nor could we use them in any way with the evacuation tasks, as my own experience at Solo sometime earlier had shown. Nevertheless we put them in the picture as well as we could.

Some days later Brian Macnamara walked over to see me after landing. He looked very hot and weary and, I thought, rather depressed.

'Well,' he said, 'the Solo job is finished. There were only 14 passengers for us today. Your friend, General Subidio, was there and he came over to see me. 'All finish: you go home', was what he said, which I thought was a pretty polite way of thanking us.'

'You didn't expect to be thanked, did you Brian?'

'No, I suppose not,' as he slumped into my chair.

'Your squadron has done remarkably well and you haven't lost or injured a single one of those passengers. We will know eventually how many you have carried out but it certainly runs into many thousands. Get as many of your chaps out swimming on the beaches and at 'Eden Island' as you can, now that the workload is slowing down. They deserve a little leisure before the future of the squadron is known. Now, let's go out and have a good Chinese dinner to-night to celebrate the most difficult part of the job.'

We did just that and, by the end of the evening, Brian was his old cheerful self again. But I could tell that he was worried about the future of his squadron. We didn't have long to wait for the answer to that question.

The news came through that his squadron was to leave us but not for disbandment. It was a fine old squadron which had spent much of its early life in India and was now destined to be reconstituted and return there, remaining as a transport squadron. Under Brian's leadership it had had a remarkable record in Java. I am not a great one for statistics but some, like these, beg to be recorded. As far as we could tell, in the past ten months the squadron had flown more than 11,000 sorties in 24,000 flying hours. Its Dakotas had carried almost 129,000 passengers of whom at least 5000 were casualties as well as lifting 26,000 tons of freight. When all the difficulties are taken into account, this was a truly remarkable achievement. During the period, the squadron lost two aircraft and, sadly, a total of 15 officers and airmen. Some of these casualties were aircrew in the Dakotas but others were airmen murdered in Batavia or shot while on duty on the airfield. Admittedly it was by far the biggest squadron in the Wing but, even so, these were grievous losses for a squadron doing a purely humanitarian job after the war was over. With these losses in mind, I must make mention of the memorial to them.

One day my Engineering Officer came to tell me that the airmen had made a memorial tablet in memory of all those who had lost their lives while serving with 904 Wing. It took the form of a polished wooden background, made from some type of local hardwood, not unlike teak, on which was mounted a copper plate with the following inscription:-

IN PROUD MEMORY OF THE MEN OF 904 WING
WHO LOST THEIR LIVES ON ACTIVE SERVICE
IN JAVA – OCTOBER 1945-46.

The plate was surmounted by the Royal Air Force eagle as worn on the shoulders of the airmen. It contained the ranks, names and units of the 32 men who had died during our stay in the island, and the engraving had been done by a Javanese craftsman.

The memorial was beautifully made in our own makeshift workshops, a truly fitting tribute. I was very touched by this quite unsolicited memorial as its construction had been carefully kept from me, but it must have represented many hours of patient and skilful work. What was the most suitable way in which to preserve it for posterity? I gave a lot of thought to this, at first wondering whether or not it should be taken home, but then I decided to form a small committee of our chaplain and those who had made it. The consensus of opinion was that it should remain in the Far East where the men had died and were buried. This was the decision we took. The padre said that, until we left Java, he would like to dedicate it and place it in his small chapel. When we departed and 904 Wing was disbanded, he would put it in the care of the Assistant

Chaplain-in-Chief in Singapore until I returned from my home leave, when a suitable resting place could be found for it. It was pointed out that many of the names on the Roll of Honour came from units which would still be serving in Singapore or India and would doubtless like to have it within South East Asia. After a service of dedication on a Sunday in August, it was given temporary resting place in our chapel. So many officers and airmen came to the Service of Dedication that the padre had to hold it outside the chapel as it was quite impossible to accommodate them all inside.

All this raised the question of what should be done with the bodies of those buried in Kemajoran. As a consequence of the near disaster of our first funeral in the public cemetery, we had been compelled to make a plot of land available within the security of the station. This was most unsatisfactory, muddy and badly drained but the best we could do at the time. Simple wooden crosses had been made and placed at the head of each grave. We could not possible leave them there and they deserved a better resting place. Once again the padre decided to invoke the help of the Assistant Chaplain-in-Chief and he flew down to us in the daily schedule flight. I was greatly relieved when he said that they must be moved, in the first place, to Singapore. He made a careful note of all the names and promised to get in touch with the next of kin to obtain their wishes. It was not official policy at that time to fly bodies home for burial and he hoped that they could be laid to rest in a military cemetery in Singapore. At the time he agreed to take care of our memorial plaque until I returned and could arrange where it should be placed.

Thoughout August the steady reduction of the Wing continued. As officers and airmen were posted home on release and left us, they were not replaced by new arrivals. This created some difficulties, but more Dutchmen came in to fill some of the vacancies and be trained in their new duties. 60 Squadron's Thunderbolts, augmented by the Dutch Mitchells, coped admirably with the protection of the road convoys and, although this protection had to be maintained well into September, the hostile action gradually died down and no more offensive air attacks were required.

I took this opportunity to get in some flying in my Thunderbolt as I knew that there would be no more chances to fly this delightful aircraft after I left Java. Each morning when I could spare the time I took off and spent up to an hour enjoying the cool part of the day with some high altitude flying. On one of these trips I paid a final visit to Bandoeng to inspect the last of RAPWI's tasks. There were now very few people to be evacuated and we were slowly closing down our operation there and bringing out some of the British soldiers who had occupied the town, and like 904 Wing, were now in the process of handing over to the Dutch.

The first Dutch naval units began to arrive as part of the arrangement. They tied up in Tanjoeng Priok docks which, by this time, were in full working order although the wrecked buildings still showed the results of the ammunition ship explosion of a year ago. I was invited to go to lunch one Sunday aboard the *Heemskerk*. She was a destroyer which had, I believe, escaped from the Netherlands and played her part with the Allies during the war.

I was entertained to liberal doses of Bols gin, followed by a superb 'reisstaffel' which went on for hours, fortified with more Bols. Dutch naval officers seemed to be capable of absorbing this fiery liquid with little or no effect and I vaguely remember staggering down a gangway which seemed to have shrunk in size since I came aboard, and drove myself slowly and carefully back to the Mess, thankful for my dark sunglasses in the glare of the afternoon sun. No more heavy parties of Bols gin, I decided.

Jackie Wales had been commanding 60 Squadron since the day I took command of the Wing in India, but I had seen little of him as the squadron had been in Soerabaya for most of our stay in Java. Now, however, he came to see me one morning. 'I would like to do a squadron formation flight around the neighbourhood before we finally depart, and I wonder whether you would like to lead it. It would bring back memories of when you were in the squadron in India: that was about twelve years ago, wasn't it?'

'I would love to do that, Jackie,' I said, 'if you think that the squadron would manage to follow some possible erratic leadership, but I must tell you that the last time I followed a station commander leading 60 was almost a disaster. It was indeed 12 years ago and our leader attempted a formation landing of nine aircraft on our airfield which was no more than about 800 yards square. He brought us in to land much too slowly with the result that nobody could stay behind him and we all had to open up and leave him isolated in the middle of the airfield. He was not a little annoyed when he came to rest, looked round and found nobody there, with Wapitis going in every direction above him. We left that to our Flight Commanders to sort out with him later. We don't want any repetition of that.'

'Well,' said Jackie, 'there's little risk of that as we can't land in formation here. The squadron would be very pleased if you would lead us round; I suggest over the city and up to Bandoeng and back.'

We agreed the route and speed – an indicated 280 – which seemed the most suitable, with nine aircraft in three flights and myself out in front. We fixed the day and I decided to inform the Air Commodore in case he could see any political objections to this great 'display of force.' He had none and thought it would do the locals good to see that our Thunderbolts were still in evidence.

One more practice flight by myself to fly over the agreed route and check on my own ability to maintain a steady 280 with wide and steady turns to accommodate the formation which would be behind me. Not too bad, I thought. The appointed day dawned, bright and windless and the nine aircraft of the squadron took off in quick succession. I followed the last one down the runway and watched them begin to form up in the distance. It was agreed that they would join me over the docks. When they began to turn left, I started a turn inside them so that they could catch me at the appointed place, heading back towards Kemajoran at 3000 feet.

All went well and Jackie called that they were catching me up more or less in formation. With 280 on the clock at 3000 feet I called the control tower for permission to overfly and received the all clear. Most of the airmen seemed to be on the tarmac as we swept over, and I hoped the squadron had got into a good formation. After telling Jackie I was turning right, a gentle turn took us over the city and close to Tjililitan. Another wide sweep and back over Kemajoran on course for Bandoeng. I then ordered a climb to 5000 feet as there was some higher ground in front and, 20 minutes later we overflew the Bandoeng airfield and the town itself. Turning gently to the left, we set course for Batavia again and, with the high ground behind, dropped to 3000 feet once more.

A final pass over the airfield when I radioed my intention of breaking upwards, leaving Jackie to cope with the rest. Opening the throttle, I pulled steadily up a couple of thousand feet, turned over to the left and watched the formation sweep past below. Their formation looked excellent, as I gathered later it had been throughout. Dropping down into the circuit, I landed and taxied in.

As I sat in the cockpit switching things off, the formation came across once more and broke up into the three flights and landed individually at very regular intervals. It was reckoned to have been a good exercise, Jackie Wales was pleased with it and I was grateful to have been asked to lead it. The troops, having their 'char and wads' clustered round Miep and her tea wagon had also enjoyed a free display and, if not complimentary, seemed to think that 'for a Group Captain' I had not done too badly. I even enjoyed Miep's tea as I cooled down.

The sight of Miep, who had now served tea and driven her wagon for ten months, reminded me of something I had had in mind for a while. As she drove away I spoke to the airmen before they drifted back to work, saying that I thought we ought to give the half dozen girls who had worked for us a present of some kind before we left. We had, of course, paid them all a modest wage but they had been so conscientious that a memento of their stay with 904 Wing seemed appropriate. I was pleased to find that some of my old hands had already had the same thought. I suggested that I should arrange for half a dozen RAF brooches to be bought in Singapore and given to the girls towards the end of our stay, together with a suitable gratuity. This proved popular and George Rumsey had six silver RAF wings bought which were then presented at a little ceremony before I left the Wing. We had employed these girls initially to get them out of Adek Camp, thus giving a few of the inmates their first taste of freedom. They proved, however, to be so useful and efficient that they took a considerable workload off the officers and airmen. One of them in particular, whose name was, I think, Ilse, was quite invaluable at co-ordinating intelligence reports and recording operational statistics in our small and extremely busy Operational Centre.

I felt that the time had now come for me to think seriously about my own home leave and when would be a suitable time to hand over command of the remnants of 904 Wing which was now rapidly disintegrating before my eyes. I decided to go and discuss the matter with Air Commodore Stevens and, with his approval, make a plan for my departure.

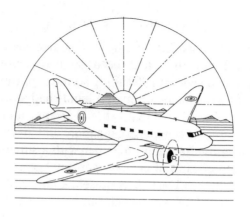

19

The End at Last

Air Commodore Stevens was in a very cheerful mood when I went to see him to discuss my home leave and other things. He told me that General Mansergh had decreed that all British forces were to be out of Java before the end of November and that we should start slimming down at once, leaving only such equipment as was essential to enable the Dutch to operate efficiently.

'It has taken us a year,' he said, 'to rescue all the prisoners and internees, far longer than was ever anticipated, but the hostile situation which we met wasn't expected either. Army casualties have been dreadful and your Wing has suffered grievous losses also. But the job has been done and we can all go home, thank God.'

He continued by saying that it would be a good thing if the Dutch, who were appointing a Colonel to be the future

Commanding Officer at Kemajoran, began to take control of much of the station as soon as possible. He suggested that I should make my own arrangements to leave during September, and my Wing Commander could remain in command until the Dutch Colonel was ready to take over.

'I'm sorry to hear that you'll have to drop a rank but it's inevitable. Hughie Edwards will do the same and you will both find yourselves in very good company throughout the Service which has already dropped from one and a quarter million to something like three or four hundred thousand in eighteen months. We have hardly noticed it here in Java as we have had to continue the war, but the RAF has really been emasculated elsewhere.'

After discussing a few more details, I left the Air Commodore and spent a few moments in Hughie's office on my way out. We commiserated with one another on the prospect of losing our ranks but, privately, I reckoned that if he, with a Victoria Cross, a DSO and a DFC was going to lose his, I hadn't too much to grumble about.

A few days later Os van Delden, the KLM manager, rang me up and asked me to lunch with him at the Hotel des Indes.

'I have a proposition to make to you,' he said somewhat mysteriously, and I readily accepted.

Knowing my Dutch friend's propensity for Bols gin I took my Corporal driver to look after the Buick and to take me safely home after lunch. After the inevitable Bols or two, van Delden said:

'My company is most grateful for the service that has been given to us during the past months. We could not have restarted our Far East route without your help. I have been authorised to offer you a job with KLM when you return to Europe if that would interest you. It would not be as a pilot but on our executive staff.'

Naturally this came as quite a shock to me, and I had to think quickly about what was clearly a most attractive proposition. KLM was one of the oldest and most professional airlines, as I had every reason to know, and their scheduled service from Amsterdam which had now risen to two per week, ran with clockwork regularity and efficiency. Was I tempted? Well, not really as my host waited for my reply. I was a regular officer and reckoned that I had a reasonable career in front of me in the Service which I loved. Also I enjoyed my flying and felt that the future offered me many more flying appointments.

'Excuse me,' I said, 'for being so long in replying to your most attractive offer.' He nodded in understanding. 'You have taken me completely by surprise. I have no thought of leaving the RAF at the moment. This job is almost over and I will be going on to another one in Singapore. In spite of the severe reductions in the size of the RAF, I feel that I have an assured future and that I should stay with my Service, but yours is an offer which I appreciate enormously, and I am most grateful to you and KLM for making it.'

'Well,' he replied. 'I'm not really surprised or upset. I have seen Kemajoran at work now for almost a year and I do admire the work which has been done there, not least in taking on the added burden of our Skymasters. Now, I have another proposal to make.'

I waited in some trepidation for this one, having turned down his first.

'I know that you will shortly be going home on leave and my company would like to offer you a passage back to England in one of our Skymasters. Our president, Mr Plesman, wants to meet and thank you in Amsterdam, and then send you on to England.'

'That,' I said immediately, 'is an offer I cannot resist and I can think of no better way to leave my station than in one of your Skymasters which have been part of our life at Kemajoran. I accept with the greatest of pleasure and many thanks.'

I need hardly say that our lunch proceeded with more Bols and great cheer. It was left to me to decide when I could conveniently hand over the Wing and van Delden said that he would then arrange for my passage as close to that date as the KLM schedules would allow.

On reflection I knew that I had made a very rapid decision to turn down the attractive offer of employment with KLM. It would undoubtedly have been some form of managerial position, perhaps in London, and it would probably have brought its financial rewards. But I knew I was right. The RAF had been my life for sixteen years; I loved it, with the excitement and challenges which it offered and, at the age of 34, I was reluctant to give up flying which would certainly have been necessary. Yes, I was sure of my decision and it was clear that van Delden fully expected me to make it. He had the offer of the flight home up his sleeve, and I could think of no more comfortable way of rejoining Denise and my family.

60 Squadron was now the only operational flying unit left at Kemajoran, fully occupied with looking after the road convoys, but even that was reduced when it was decided to detach one Flight to take over the last few duties in Sumatra where the Spitfire squadron, which had been at Medan since the beginning of the occupation, was to be disbanded.

After talking things over with my few remaining officers, I decided that I could hand over and leave in about ten days time, that was, in mid-September. The new Dutch Commanding Officer had made himself known to me – a thoroughly experienced air force officer who was delighted at the prospect of his first post-war command. It was clear that we would need to leave a great deal of equipment behind to ensure that the station could continue to operate efficiently, but fortunately the financial arrangements for transferring it were out of my hands. All we had to do was to provide lists and inventories of all the items and see that they were in good condition – or as good as could be expected after twelve months of usage in the rough-and-tumble conditions of Kemajoran.

I rang van Delden, invited him to lunch with me this time and told him that I could take advantage of his offer of a passage at any time in the next week or two. I also invited the Dutch colonel in order to introduce him to van Delden who would be working with him after the hand over. We met as before at the

Hotel des Indes and van Delden told me that I could join the KLM flight due to leave Kemajoran on 10th September.

'One of our most experienced pilots, Captain Bott, will be taking that flight and I know you will get on well with him. He has been here several times in recent months and appreciated what your Wing has done for us.'

This gave me seven days in which to make my final arrangements and warn Denise that I would soon be on my way, expecting to reach home on about the 14th. It was a splendid way to finish my tour, much better than taking a Dakota to Singapore and awaiting a Transport Command flight in a York to England.

After making my arrangements known to the Air Commodore and to the headquarters in Singapore, I received a signal to the effect that I was to return to Singapore after my leave – as a Wing Commander – and to take up the appointment of Wing Commander Administrative Plans. Oh well! I could cope with that for the remaining year or so of my tour, but I was certainly going to leave Kemajoran as a fully fledged Group Captain – battered hat and all. I didn't tell anybody, therefore, about the signal I had received. 'Let them find out in due course,' I thought.

After a round of farewells, not unaccompanied by many glasses of Bols, the day of departure arrived – 10th September, 1946. The KLM Skymaster was drawn up on the tarmac, and I was delighted to see that it was by coincidence, NL300, the same aircraft which had inaugurated the Far East service ten months earlier and in which I had flown to Bandoeng with Captain Parmentier. Captain Bott was now in command and I had met him the previous evening when saying goodbye to van Delden. Bott was one of KLM's long serving pilots with many thousands of hours in his log book.

I climbed aboard after waving to a crowd of my officers and airmen who gathered on the tarmac on this bright sunny morning. Six Thunderbolts had just taken off and I had watched them climb away, with some feeling of nostalgia, knowing that I would never have the pleasure of flying one again. My own was still standing on the grass outside the hanger, looking rather scruffy and forlorn. This was also my last drive in my straight eight Buick which now had to be handed over to the Dutch colonel – lucky man; it was a fine car and had been kept immaculately by my Corporal driver. Captain Bott invited me to take the co-pilot's seat and we taxied out with waves and salutes from my colleagues. For the last time, down that Bit Hess runway which had stood up so well to almost a year's hard use. I wondered as we gathered speed what our Dutch successors would manage to do with it as it obviously could not continue in that state indefinitely, with no Japanese prisoners-of-war to stick it down again after almost every landing.

We circled round once to let me have a last look at Kemajoran and the city before setting course and climbing out to sea over the docks. A few moments later I looked out of my right hand window to see a formation of three Thunderbolts creeping up alongside. Bott touched my arm and pointed towards the other window where three more were in position – a farewell escort by 60 Squadron.

Bott said to me over the intercom, 'Speak to them, we are on the same frequency.' Knowing their call sign, I spoke to the squadron and at once recognised Jackie Wales' voice in reply. We spoke for a few moments and I thanked them for the escort and wished him and his squadron good luck for the future. With a wave of his hand which I could clearly see under his canopy, the two flights drew ahead of us and, when well clear, climbed steeply and fell away to right and to left. That was the last time I saw a Thunderbolt as all 60 Squadron's aircraft were broken up before the squadron disbanded in November, to be reformed on Spitfires in Singapore. When they had gone I said to Bott:

'I must apologise for their breaking all the rules of civil aviation.'

'Not to worry,' he replied, 'I arranged it all with your squadron commander who asked my permission yesterday. It was a nice gesture and the least I could do was to agree.'

It was indeed a nice gesture, and I was touched by it. My feelings were very mixed; joy at going home to the family and relief at coming to the end of what had been quite a traumatic experience, but some sadness at leaving 904 Wing which had proved such a fine command for the past eighteen months. Was it really only eighteen months? It seemed like years.

Captain Bott realised that I was brooding over events and said briskly, 'You take over and fly to Singapore. You know the way. Keep her at 8000 feet and our co-pilot will take my seat and keep an eye on you. I'm going to have a cup of coffee with the passengers.'

That jerked me back to the job in hand as he left the flight deck and his young Dutch co-pilot squeezed himself between the seats and took his captain's position. A few moments later, as I was approaching 8,000 feet, the cabin door opened and one of the stewardesses came with face flannels soaked in eau de cologne, and proceeded to wipe our overheated faces. This was a little touch which was repeated after every take-off in the tropics and very welcome it was.

At our cruising altitude, the automatic pilot was engaged and I was able to relax and keep an eye on the instruments. It was an extremely steady and accurate automatic pilot, the weather was calm and smooth with the sun shining brilliantly on the sea below as we passed by the thousand islands.

Captain Bott returned to the cockpit some time later in order to take over control as we approached Singapore.

'We will not stop for more than 45 minutes at Kallang. A quick refuel and load six more passengers and then on to Bangkok which takes about five hours, and I try to get there in daylight for the sake of the passengers.'

The flight from Batavia had taken three and a quarter hours, slightly less than a Dakota would take. The RAF had left Kallang which was now a purely civil airport, and not at all a satisfactory one as the air liners using it got larger and faster. Pilots hated the sea wall at one end of the runway, knowing that if they overshot, a main road awaited them at the other end. It did not, however, seem to worry our captain who put the Skymaster down with the greatest precision.

We were soon on our way again and, for this leg, I took my seat in the cabin while our co-pilot flew most of the way. I told Captain Bott that I hoped I wasn't intruding when on the flight deck but he assured me he was happy for me to take a turn at the controls. 'Johannes (the co-pilot) and I get quite enough flying and we don't mind the occasional break from it.'

'How many hours have you done?' I asked.

'Oh, about 13,000.'

That made my 2000 odd hours look a little insignificant and so I kept fairly quiet on the subject. Five and a half hours later we landed at Bangkok as the light was fading. There was, however, enough left to get a good view of the many splendid Buddhist temples and the waterways which are such a feature of the city. Dinner with the crew, who always dressed smartly during their overnight stops, followed by an early night in a first class hotel – my first night away from the discomforts of Kemajoran for a long time. Already thoughts of 904 Wing were beginning to be overtaken by the anticipation of getting home, and I fell asleep thinking of the welcome which I knew would await me.

The next day was a long one, more than 12 hours in the air to Karachi with a brief refuelling stop at Calcutta. It was dark when we landed but I wasn't very interested as my last acquaintance with Karachi had been boarding a most uncomfortable troopship at the end of a long tour of duty in 1936, almost exactly 10 years earlier to the day.

Our third day was even longer, more than 13 hours flying, of which I flew the Skymaster for about five between Karachi and Basrah which, even in September, was unbearably hot in the middle of the day. We were all glad to climb away over the Iraqi desert towards Cairo, our next night stop. The eau de cologne flannels were more welcome than ever as they were brought up to the flight deck with the dust, sand and heat of Basrah left behind.

Travelling west, we were of course, gaining time, if one can express it that way, so that, even after 14 hours since our dawn take-off, it was still daylight as we descended over Cairo. But it had been a tiring day and I was more than ready for a cooler night's sleep. The next day would see the aircraft home in Amsterdam although I still had to get across the Channel. However KLM had offered me a passage to England, and I could safely leave the arrangements to them. I would dearly like to have treated the crew to some champagne at dinner that evening, but my proposal was a mistake.

'Sorry,' said Captain Bott, 'we never drink when we are flying. It's a pity, but thank you very much for the offer.'

With the four engines running as sweetly as they had throughout, we headed for Rome, the last stop on the last day. The European weather was not good and we battled our way through heavy cloud for six hours before dropping through to a rainswept Ciampino airport at Rome. I had been in tropical uniform as far as Cairo and, although I had a blue uniform with me, it had not seen the light of day for eighteen months and was creased and scruffy. When our captain told me that he had received a signal to the effect that Mr Plesman, the President of KLM, would like to see me in the morning after we reached Amsterdam, I had to do something about it. An Egyptian chambermaid came to my rescue and took the uniform off to be sponged and pressed. It came back looking reasonably presentable but nothing could be done about the terrible hat, and Mr Plesman would have to be understanding.

During the final leg of the flight I sat in my cabin seat and enjoyed the luxury of a first class passenger. The view of the Alps was superb, the higher peaks being covered with the first snow of the autumn bathed in sunshine. I dozed off and woke to find Captain Bott sitting beside me.

'I've just received a signal to say that a car will be taking you to an hotel, and also to take you to see Mr Plesman at 9 o'clock tomorrow morning. He will tell you what arrangements have been made to fly you home tomorrow.'

THE END AT LAST

I thanked him and, in particular, for allowing me to share the flight deck with him.

'We were delighted,' he replied, 'with three pilots we have never had a more restful trip.'

With that pleasantry he went back to the job of getting us safely into Schipol at Amsterdam. It was 6 o'clock when the Skymaster finally touched down at one of the busiest airports in Europe, and it was time for me to say goodbye to the crew which had looked after me so well for four days. Java and 904 Wing now seemed a very long way away, and I would gladly have gone home that evening had it been possible.

A member of the KLM staff met me and took me to my hotel for the night, telling me that everything was on KLM and I was to have a first class dinner, a good night's rest and he would collect me on the following morning.

Mr Plesman came across his sumptuous office to meet me and we had a long chat over coffee. He was very complimentary over the help that 904 Wing had given his company.

'Without the help of the RAF all down the route in 1945,' he said, 'we could not possibly have started our Far East route for many months.'

I thanked him for the generous offer which van Delden had made to me on his behalf.

'It was a tempting offer but I feel that, as a regular officer, my future lies with the RAF.'

'I think you made a wise decision,' he replied, 'you are obviously well established in your career and these post-war years are not the time to change unless it's essential. Now, if you can remember your home telephone number, you can ring up your wife from here' – pointing to his phone – 'and say that you will be landing at Croydon at 4.30 this evening, complete with a basket of strawberries for her and the the thanks of KLM.'

As I rose to go Mr Plesman said, 'I don't wish to seem rude, but where did you get that hat?'

'Damn: I hoped you wouldn't notice that. It was made by an Indian tailor in Delhi eighteen months ago and has been an embarrassment to me ever since, but it was impossible to replace it in Java. This is the very last time I will have to wear it.'

He laughed, shook me by the hand and said,

'Well, it certainly shows that it has had to work for its living.'

By one o'clock I was climbing into a highly polished silver KLM Dakota with comfortable seats, very different from the Dakotas we had in Java with tin benches along the sides of the cabin which folded up against the sides to accommodate freight – or dried fish.

Two and a half hours later, Central London was below us and within five minutes, the wheels gently touched the grass of Croydon airport. Carrying my large basket of strawberries, I quickly passed through customs and there was Denise to meet me. It was a happy end to a strange tour of duty and a great sense of relief came over me as I realised that at last my war was over.

Postscript

My story has ended, but one essential duty remained to be done when I returned to Singapore after my home leave. A suitable resting place had to be found for the 904 Wing memorial plaque. My final duty to my Wing was to ensure that it remained for posterity where it would be seen and respected, not only by those who had served in Java, but by future generations of airmen.

I arrived back at Changi after a tedious journey which took seven days, firstly, by RAF York aircraft and finally in a Sunderland flying boat from Ceylon, the last part of the journey taking more than eleven hours at low level in very turbulent conditions. Not as comfortable as my homeward journey had been. Christmas was soon upon us and I deeply regretted that I had not been able to stay and enjoy it with my

223

family, but my leave was up and my orders to return had been explicit.

The Assistant Chaplain-in-Chief had the memorial safely in his care, cleaned and polished, and we discussed where it could appropriately be placed.

'I have thought about it,' he said, 'and I feel that the best place is in the station church at Tengah. As you know, Tengah is our main operational station and two of your 904 Wing squadron group are there. I think we should go and look at the church and you can make up your mind.'

We drove over to Tengah, in the middle of Singapore island, some time later and, with the station padre, went to see the church. It was a small stone building which I understood had been built by prisoners-of-war. I liked it at once and we all agreed there and then that it was an ideal place. The memorial could be mounted on the back wall, to the left of the entrance where it could be in full view of congregations leaving the church. I took this opportunity to call on my two old squadrons, 60 and 81, which still contained many of the Java boys, and they were all enthusiastic at the idea of having their plaque on their station – and so that was that.

It only remained for a suitable installation Service to be arranged. The Commander-in-Chief, still Air Marshal Sir George Pirie, said that he would be very pleased to attend and unveil the memorial. We finally settled on a date – March 9th, 1947.

I shall not forget that simple and impressive Service. The church was crowded and the Assistant Chaplain-in-Chief preached a moving and appropriate sermon, after which Sir George Pirie unveiled the plaque which was then dedicated. It looked splendid, highly polished and flanked by the original RAF and Dutch flags which had been hoisted at Kemajoran. Before the end of the Service I gave a short address from the chancel steps in which I identified all the individual names on the plaque and briefly stated how they lost their lives.

I finished by saying that, although our RAF losses had been grievous, we must not forget that the British Army lost many more soldiers in Java but, in so doing, tens of thousands of our prisoners of war and internees had been rescued from the appalling conditions in which they had been kept for years. Those who had lost their lives had done so in a great humanitarian cause.

The congregation was completely silent as I finished my address and I could not help but feel that even those in Singapore, let alone those at home, had never fully understood the extraordinary situation which had continued in Java for more than a year after the capitulation of Japan.